Joseph M. Brown

Kennesaw's Bombardment

How the sharpshooters woke up the batteries

Joseph M. Brown

Kennesaw's Bombardment
How the sharpshooters woke up the batteries

ISBN/EAN: 9783337328757

Printed in Europe, USA, Canada, Australia, Japan

Cover: Foto ©ninafisch / pixelio.de

More available books at **www.hansebooks.com**

KENNESAW'S BOMBARDMENT,

OR

How the Sharpshooters Woke up the Batteries.

BY

JOSEPH M. BROWN.

Atlanta, Ga.
Record Publishing Company.
1890.

PREFACE.

It is customary for an author to introduce his book with a preface, and, since
"Man yields to custom as he bows to fate,"
this book will have to begin with a preface, although it has become necessary to drop out a few shells in order to get it in, the only regret of the "men who were on the mountain top," being that the omission was not made over twenty-five years earlier.

As the reader will readily gather by wading through it, and looking at the pictures, it is intended as a historical novel,—as a view of the panorama which war spread out upon and around Kennesaw Mountain on that "day of thrilling events,"—the historical part of it being as nearly correct as it is possible to make it by laboriously and carefully fishing out the facts with a drag-net with pin-hook attachment,— and the fictitious part being as fascinating as the writer's riotous love of sentiment will allow. If it be urged by the northern reader that the "sentiment" is all southern, it is a fair reply to say that that was the kind which prevailed on Kennesaw at the date shown in the book; and the author's intention and determination have been to make the picture a true and characteristic one.

In the preparation of this work, there has been the most extensive research, at odd times within the past three years, through official reports, files of daily newspapers published during June, 1864, and correspondence or personal conversations with those who took part in the scenes attempted to be described. All the characters in the book are real ones, except some four or five, and those the reader, whether he has got his "Counterfeit Detector" with him or not, will doubtless readily pick out.

There are several anachronisms as to dates, none, however, being actually more than three or four days before or after June 23, and the incidents in question are all brought into that day for the purpose of making it illustrate what was practically the everyday experience during the almost two weeks that the Confederate batteries were on the mountain-top.

Of course there had to be a pretty girl in it, or else the novel would not have been a stunning success, no matter whether the bombardment was or not.

Atlanta, Ga., January 15, 1890.

KENNESAW'S BOMBARDMENT,

— OR —

How the Sharpshooters Woke up the Batteries.

CHAPTER I.

It was on the forenoon of Thursday, June 23d, 1864.

A cold, drenching rain had been falling many hours. The two weeks of wet weather had culminated in a furious thunderstorm; and the past night and this morning had seemed to gather unto themselves almost the terrific grandeur of a tropical tempest. Rain! rain! rain! the forests were dropping it like spray, the hillsides were shedding it in sheets, the creeks were becoming rivers.

But the center of all the elements' fury was Kennesaw Mountain. About its twin peaks the clouds had clustered as though they were a storm magnet. The lightning, which occasionally flashed its dazzling splendors through the blinding darkness of the night, seemed to blaze around the towering crests like a fiery diadem; the thunder, which rolled forth and reverberated with deafening echoes for leagues around, one could almost imagine was the wrathful shout of the mountain god. How the winds howled! how the rain poured!

Thus through the night the aerial battle had raged; and with scarcely less fury had it continued until well into the forenoon.

At length, as if from the mere exhaustion of the elements, a calm hour came on. The rain ceased falling, except now and then a light mist, which, observed from the valley, appeared like a veil to adorn the mountain. Then through a rift in the storm-cloud a golden shaft seemed to dart; and the next instant the mountain top was glorified by a halo of dazzling sun-light. Then the drifting fog enveloped it again, and obscurity was lord for a minute.

But the fresh breeze, which had just sprung up, soon swept away again these "cobwebs from the sky," and majestic Kennesaw's crown once more towered above the vision for miles around.

Thus alternately the flashing sunlight and the thickly-banked clouds struggled for the possession of the mountain and the surrounding hills and fields. And how similar was this war for mastery of the elements above to that which at the same time was being waged by man below, in which the grandest genius of America was giving direction to the marshalling of the bravest and most intelligent soldiery of the age.

WAKING UP THE BATTERIES.   7

But now as the storm is breaking, and the first sunshine of a fortnight* is lighting the sky, let us look immediately upon Kennesaw, for there the initial steps are just being taken which will shortly bring about one of the most thrillingly magnificent yet terrific scenes which America ever witnessed.

For nearly a month Johnston's and Sherman's armies had been fighting with desperate valor in sight of Kennesaw Mountain. New Hope Church, Pickett's Mill, Lost Mountain, Pine Mountain, Gilgal Church, Mud Creek, Noonday Creek, Brush Mountain, once names of mere local note, had now become throughout the land household synonyms for scenes of blood.

The battle front had been successively changed until to-day the Confederate army faced its enemy's almost double numbers with entrenchments which began east of the Western & Atlantic Railroad, thence crossed it, and ran up the long ridge of Kennesaw Mountain, just below the north front of both crests, and, descending its western slant, turned abruptly south, and extended through the valley and over the hills, parallel to the railroad, for some four miles.

Loring's corps (till late that of the Bishop-General

---

* "The weather is villainously bad."—Gen. Sherman to Gen. Thomas, June 18, 1864.

"This is the nineteenth day of rain, and the prospect of clear weather as far off as ever. The roads are impassable, and fields and woods become quagmires after a few wagons have crossed. * * * The enemy holds Kennesaw, a conical mountain, with Marietta behind it, and has retired his flanks to cover that town and his railroad. I am all ready to attack the moment the weather and roads will permit troops and arti'lery to move with anything like life."—Gen. Sherman to Gen. Halleck, June 21, 1864.

Polk, whose tragic death on Pine Mountain had crowned it in the Southland's memory with the immortelles of melancholy,) covered the mountain.

Walthall's division (Quarles' brigade on the right, Cantey's in the center and Reynolds' on the left,) extended from the base up the ridge of Great Kennesaw to the crest, and there met the right brigade (Ector's) of French's division, which descended to the gap between the two peaks and over the little knob which rises like a hump from the ravine between Great and Little Kennesaw. Ector's brigade also occupied the works from this ravine to the top of Little Kennesaw, thence Sears' was prolonged behind those on the north side of and a little below the summit and partly down the slope on the west, at which point it aligned with Cockrell's Missouri brigade, whose front extended down the exposed slant, across the ravine and over the high hill on the west, to the plain.

It was now well into the morning, and General French, who had come from his headquarters up to the mountain top early after breakfast, had just gotten through with a short consultation with his brigade commanders and some others, who had been afterwards called in, to join an informal discussion over the military situation that day.

Standing by a huge crag near the eastern end of the summit of Little Kennesaw was General French himself,—short in stature, but the ideal of a commander. On his right, on a rock, sat Colonel W. S. Barry, who was in command of the brigade

WAKING UP THE BATTERIES.   9

of General Sears, who was absent this day because of sickness, and by his side, writing in his note-book, was Major D. W. Sanders, General French's Adjutant-General; leaning against an artillery caisson in front, examining a map, was the tall form of General Francis M. Cockrell, every inch a soldier; with him stood Lieutenant-Colonel D. Todd Samuels, of the Third Missouri cavalry, and on the other side, Colonel James McCown, of the Fifth Missouri, was reading a memorandum order which had just been handed him by Colonel Elijah Gates, the gallant and popular commander of the First Missouri cavalry, and Cockrell's chief lieutenant.

Standing on the rocky parapet in front of one of the cannon of Hoskins' battery,—whose muzzle faced Pine Mountain, where was now a Federal signal station,—Colonel W. H. Young, of the Ninth Texas cavalry, with a field-glass was surveying the movements of a body of Federal infantry from the vicinity of the Cheatham house on the north toward the mountain.

By his side was Major Geo. S. Storrs, General French's chief of artillery, who had been called by some, "one of the bravest men in the Confederate army," under whose direction the Confederates had planted several batteries on the crest of the mountain. This achievement was one almost wonderful in the boldness of its conception, and the ingenuity and triumph over the apparently insurmountable obstacles which nature had placed in the way.

The fire from the Federal batteries commanding

the slanting end of the mountain, he had found a way to drag the cannon by men with long ropes,—there being two hundred men allotted to each cannon, in performing this task,—up the steep side on the south; and here now, from behind the monstrous bowlders, or piles of loose stones, they frowned upon the Federal camps and works in the plain and on the hills far below.

These parapets were erected by General Gibson's Louisiana Brigade, which was temporarily attached to French's division, being on this date, with Holtzclaw's Alabama Brigade, in reserve behind the mountain. Of General Gibson and his command Major Storrs said: "The artillerymen thought him a very clever gentleman and his brigade fine soldiers, because all they asked of us was to set the stakes, and then they went energetically at it with picks and shovels, and not only built splendid works, but carried by hand a large amount of ammunition up the mountain and stored it in our extempore magazines, while the artillerymen, except a few to give directions, slept so as to be fresh for the next day."

Of Major Storrs himself the most characteristic description probably was given by one of the artillerymen of Captain Hoskins' detachment on the mountain top, when asked who was in command of that section of Hoskins' battery—the captain himself being in personal charge of that section which was on the hill to the west of Kennesaw. Said he: "I cannot say who was in command, unless it was

PLANTING THE GUNS ON KENNESAW.

Major Storrs, who, in person, gave us every order we received on the mountain. He was about as near one of us as could be, and often sighted and directed the movement of the guns. In fact, he was everywhere where things were the warmest. He was over the mountain constantly every day, and I never saw a time anything was being shot away, but what Major Storrs was in sight or near by. Yes, he was a good one, and you could bet everything you had or could borrow on his personal skill and courage. It would take a great deal of space to write up the good soldierly qualities of Major Storrs."

Right behind Major Storrs and Colonel Young, sitting on a rock and drawing a profile, were Major Gus (J. A.) Shingleur, the division Inspector General, and Captain Porter, of the engineers, who had both assisted Major Storrs in making an examination of Little Kennesaw before the guns were taken up.

Only a few steps to the left of these, two officers, subordinate in rank, but greatly beloved by officers and men alike, were engaged in earnest conversation. These were Lieutenant Archibald D. Manning, a Cumberland Presbyterian preacher, and Lieutenant F. M. Baker, of the Fifth Missouri infantry, a model officer and Christian.

In front of the parapet, about twenty steps down the mountain side, in the shadow of a tree, was a group of officers and men surveying the prospect below them extending far away on the north and west.

WAKING UP THE BATTERIES. 13

Among these were Colonel W. H. Clark, of the Forty-sixth Mississippi regiment, (Sears' brigade), Colonel J. L. Camp, of the Fourteenth Texas, Colonel D. Coleman, of the Thirty-ninth North Carolina, Major H. D. E. Redwine,—the latter three belonging to Ector's brigade, and Captain A. J. Booty, of the Fourteenth Texas.

Sitting on a crag, just to the left, were Captain Pat Canniff, brave and shrewd, and Lieutenant J. R. Mothershead, a most gallant officer and exemplary Christian gentleman. These belonged to Cockrell's brigade.

Farther up to the left was a group of artillery officers, among whom was Captain Jno. J. Ward, whose gallantry and wisdom as an officer were matched by his genial disposition and estimable social qualities; although the crowning trait of his character was his pure Christian love. As was said of him, "he was every inch a soldier, every inch a gentleman." By his side Captain James A. Hoskins was engaged in a jocular dispute with Captain R. H. Bellamy over the relative superiority of the ten-pounder Parrott guns which were in their respective batteries.

"That's very good for bragging," exclaimed Captain C. L. Lumsden, who with Captain Bellamy had left their respective batteries down the west slope of the hill at the end of the mountain, commanding the Burnt Hickory road from Marietta, and come up here in obedience to orders, to join in a consultation with General French and Major

Storrs; "but my Alabama battery of Napoleons would make both of you jump for cover if I opened upon you."

"Ha! ha! wait till you hear from the proprietor of Guibor's Missouri battery," interjected Lieutenant A. W. Harris, of that battery, "and you'll think there's thunder among the mountains."

"Well, the Lord knows we don't want any more thunder among the mountains," exclaimed a private, who was burnishing his gun, "especially if it fetches as much rain as it did last night. Gracious! it seemed like Niagaray Falls, as the Vermont Yankee called 'em, was a pouring down on me, as I stood on picket duty near the foot of the mountain. I think enough water soaked into me to dilute all the whisky I'll drink for a month. I didn't want to stay down there in it five minutes, but the trouble was I had an engagement to stay there all night; and it was like an engagement to be hung,—one which couldn't be dispensed with without danger of serious detriment to the public interest."

"Boys," said Lieutenant Mothershead, who had heard this last remark, "I have been told about being enfolded in the arms of Morpheus; but last night all of us were enfolded in the arms of the thunderstorm. Why, our tent was worth no more than a veil. The clouds rolled against it so thick that you could feel them with the hand; the rain beat in like it was coming through a sieve, and, to cap it all, a gust of wind came howling along and tore it entirely from the pins on one side. Just

WAKING UP THE BATTERIES. 15

then the lightning seemed to set the whole mountain on fire, and the peal of thunder that followed is almost roaring in my ears yet."

"Well, there's some consolation about it all," exclaimed Captain Canniff, "if another flood comes it will drown the Yankees first; or it will make them come up here and surrender to us. Just imagine old Sherman's hundred thousand men climbing up the mountain to surrender to our division!"

"How did you say General Sears was?" asked General French of Colonel Barry, as they and several others walked by the group of artillery officers toward the west.

"I received a note from his headquarters only an hour ago," was the reply, "and he is reported a little better this morning."

"Well, I am glad to learn that," said General French, "but did I understand you to say that he has established his headquarters down yonder in the valley at the base of the mountain which he will have to climb?"

"Yes, sir," answered Colonel Barry, "he is down there. You know General Sears comes from Mississippi where there is not much mountain climbing."

"But," said General French, "location and accessibility to his brigade are a necessity. Send word to him that as soon as he recovers he had better move his headquarters nearer the line, the mountain is so inaccessible."

"All right, General," responded Col. Barry,

16 KENNESAW'S BOMBARDMENT.

"and as I am just sending my morning report down to him, I will add that such is your wish in the matter."

Turning to a sergeant who was with him he wrote a note and handed to him with orders to take the papers to General Sears.

CHAPTER II.

"Say, Colonel," exclaimed a North Georgia mountaineer, named Partridge, to Col. Young, "what do you make out of that body of Yankees down there in the field, near the railroad? Don't you think we could creep down the mountain, and get the range of 'em, and make 'em behave 'emselves?"

"Yes," answered the colonel, "they seem to be making observations; and it might be well to run them behind cover. Suppose you sharpshooters get down among those crags yonder, and try them."

"Well, we're the chaps to do it," sang out a Texan.

"Love is love and beauty's beauty;
But killing Yanks, ah! that is duty."

sang out a couple of others; and then the word was passed along the line that the sharpshooters would have the privilege of entertaining themselves for the next hour or two without restraint.

There were nearly twenty of these who were picked men,—selected for fine marksmanship, and furnished with good Whitworth* and Enfield rifles,

---

* "We had a corps of sharpshooters, however, perhaps the most expert in the army. They were armed with the Whitworth rifle—an English gun with a telescope on the side. This gun was deemed the best in use. Each brigade had four of them. We could not procure more. They were expensive and rare."—Benham's "Life of Gen. P. R. Cleburne."

"I heard that the Whitworth rifles cost fifteen hundred dollars a piece in gold in England, and the Yankees never had any of them. I know Porter, one of the picked men, was shot in the eye on Kennesaw or around it, and died in a few days. I shot his gun

the best which could be imported from Europe or captured from the enemy. Partridge was a volunteer member of this body, having joined the army after some of Garrard's cavalry had burned his cabin and turned his family out in the woods. He captured his own rifle, a Whitworth, from a Federal sharpshooter whom he waylaid and killed near Cassville. This identical gun had been taken from a Confederate sharpshooter (of Cheatham's division) who was mortally wounded the day before, near Adairsville. Partridge having rescued it was allowed to retain it.

They disappeared among the bushes down the mountain side, in the neighborhood of a steep, craggy formation of outcropping rocks, where there was perfect shelter from danger from shells.

"Say, Captain Ward," yelled Partridge, "if they get to shootin' b'ilin' pots at us you must show 'em that your Parrotts can say 'Pretty Poll,' too."

"Ha! ha!" laughed the captain good-humoredly, "we'll drop some shells among them if they open upon you; make that group of officers get back out of sight. They are taking too leisurely a look at us."

"All right, we'll make 'em do it, even if we have

a few days; but they kick so, and you hold a long telescope to your eye that runs along the barrel, and if you are not careful to keep it tight against the shoulder, so that when you fire your head must come back with the recoil, or else you receive the kick in your eye which would put it out. There were only five of these in our division, and they were the surest to kill of anything. The Whitworth balls are very long, and nearly all the Yankee prisoners had picked up one as a relic, saying they had killed a man or a horse a mile in the rear of their army."—Letter from a member of Hoskins' battery to the author.

WAKING UP THE BATTERIES.   19

to wake up the batteries," halloed Partridge, as he passed out of sight.

"My Parrotts, eh!" laughed Captain Ward, turning to Major Storrs, "well, Parrotts or Napoleons, they are the same to him if we will only drop a shell or so down yonder should the Yankee artillery open upon him."

"Yes," answered the major, "Partridge does not care anything about names so he gets the thing he wants. A wonderfully fine marksman he is; and we will soon hear from him."

"Why, great heavens! Minon, what does this mean?" exclaimed Captain Ward, as he walked back on the crest of the ridge, and suddenly met one of his sergeants, who was only a few steps in front of a beautiful lady and a little boy.

"Ah! Captain Ward, let me introduce you to Miss Harper, and to Master Jack Harper," said the gallant young artilleryman.

Captain Ward's polite bow was met by a most graceful one from the young lady, while little Jack came forward and extended his hand, saying, "And is this your Captain Ward, Mr. Minon? Why he's a mighty good-looking man to be a cannon man."

The captain grasped Jack's hand cordially, and answered, "Thank you, Master Jack, I am Captain Ward, the cannon man."

"Well, then, Captain Ward, I want to join your cannon company, and be one of your soldiers. I want to learn to shoot one of your biggest cannon. They make a heap of noise."

"Ha! ha! ha!" laughed the captain, "do you think you are large enough, Jack, to shoot a cannon? Then you must know that all of my soldiers have to obey orders; and I am afraid that you would want to get away if I ordered you to stay when the Yankees got to throwing big bombshells all around you."

"Oh! I'd stay if you ordered me to," answered Jack in a tone of very positive earnestness, "please, Captain, can't I be one of your soldiers?"

"Yes," said Miss Harper to the captain, "it is Jack's highest ambition to be a soldier, and shoot the cannon. He has been begging for several days to be allowed to come up on the mountain, and see the soldiers and the cannon; so last night Mr. Minon promised that if to-day was fair, he would bring Jack up. He had no idea he would be called upon to do so; but this morning after the clouds scattered, Jack summoned him to make good his promise, and, after some argument, carried his point. Mother, however, would not agree to let him come till Mr. Minon said he would take special care of him; and then I was persuaded to come along, as there was no danger to-day, and help keep him within bounds."

"And, Captain, it would have made you proud of our Georgia young ladies if you had seen how bravely Miss Harper stood the trip up the mountain side till we arrived here about a half hour ago. She did not seem to be as tired as I was."

"Oh, no, it is not a feeling of weariness, but of

WAKING UP THE BATTERIES. 21

apprehension of danger which disturbs me," said his fair comrade. "Do you think we are going to have any fighting to-day, Captain Ward?"

"Well, I hope not up here to any great extent," answered the latter, "at least for a little while yet. Come forward with me, and look over at the Yankee camps on the north and west."

"Yes, let's shoot the cannon at 'em, Captain Ward," sang out Jack.

"Come here, Miss Harper," said Captain Ward, "and let us survey the panorama which war spreads out before us. Look south now to that prominent hill which rises so conspicuously out of the plain, about two or three miles from here. That is the centre of General Cheatham's position, and is just east of the house and farm of a countryman named Channell. His division occupies a strong line of entrenchments on its crest, extends beyond it also to the south, and comes up this way for a few hundred yards until it reaches the portion of our line which is held by the gallant Pat Cleburne and his famous division.

"Ah! what heroes Cleburne and Cheatham are. They are the two lions of the Confederate army,— Cheatham combining the resistless impetuosity of a Frenchman in a charge, with the bull-dog grip of an Englishman or Russian, when told to hold a position despite whatever odds are hurled against him; and Cleburne, with the fiery gallantry of an Irishman,* as he is, in assault sweeping everything before him

* Cleburne was Irish by birth and raising, but he was of English parentage.

like a tornado; and shooting out, if I may use the comparison, the fervid heat of an iron furnace against all who attempt to penetrate whatever stronghold he is directed to occupy.

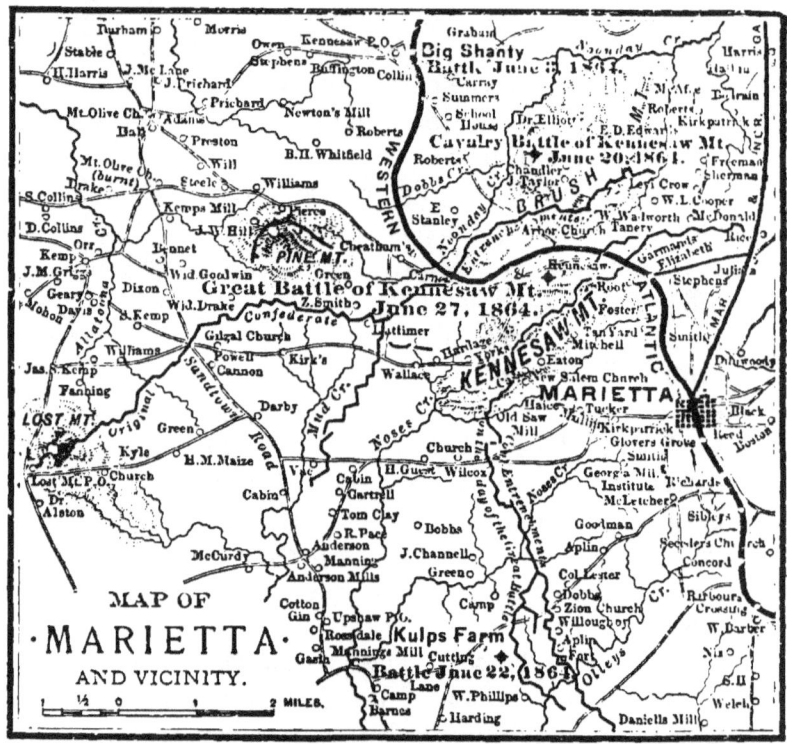

"Then beginning this side of the Marietta and Dallas wagon road, within less than a mile from here and following the line up this way, is the division of General Bate, of Tennessee; while right adjoining him, and coming up to the very foot of the mountain beneath us, is your Georgia general,

Wm. H. T. Walker, a comparatively small man in stature, but one who could give Julius Cæsar some lessons in courage if the great Roman were alive to-day. These four divisions compose General Hardee's corps.

"Then General French's division starts near the foot of the mountain and comes up to where we are, and runs along before us around the side of the mountain, and thence crosses the ravine to our right and up almost to the very summit of Great Kennesaw over yonder, where he joins General Walthall, whose courage is the admiration of the army; thence, as we go down the mountain to its base we could see, if we were on Big Kennesaw, where Featherston's division ends beyond the Western & Atlantic Railroad, and Wheeler's dismounted cavalry occupies the trenches which up to yesterday General Hood's corps have held, and which extend for nearly a mile east of here; but General Hood's command has been transferred* from

* "As the extension of the Federal army toward the Chattahoochee made a corresponding one necessary on our part, Hood's corps was transferred from the right to the Marietta and Powder Spring road, his right near the south of Cheatham's left. General Hood was instructed to endeavor to prevent any progress of the Federal right toward the railroad, the course of which was nearly parallel to our left and centre. Our position, consequently, was a very hazardous one."—Johnston's Narrative, page 339.

"Johnston had begun to be concerned for the Marietta and Powder Spring road, for Hooker's right was close to it, and Schofield's movements were threatening to put him astride of it. Hardee had stretched his lines quite as far as was safe, and the Confederate commander determined to move the whole of Hood's corps from the right to the left flank. Ordering Wheeler to show a bold front and make as strong a fight with his dismounted cavalry as he could, Johnston left these, with such help as could be got by stretching Loring's corps to the right, to fill the trenches out of which Hood was drawn. This movement was made in the night of the 21st. * * * It is uncertain to what degree Loring's corps had been extended to Johnston's right to supply the place from which Hood had been taken; but it is hardly credible that

that position to our extreme left, and occupies a line of works which run probably a mile or two southward. He had a pretty tough fight down yonder yesterday near Kolb's farm, and I am sorry to say we got the worst of it. The Yankees, you see, are swinging to their right and to our left which is south of us. They are attempting to get possession of the railroad in our rear, and all of General Johnston's anxiety now, I think, is to maintain his communications. We must protect the railroad or we cannot hold Marietta and Kennesaw Mountain."

"God grant that they may never secure a further lodgement on our State road!" said Miss Harper, "for Kennesaw, the citadel of Georgia, must be held, or the waves of war's tempest will dash around Atlanta itself."

"Yes; that is true," said Captain Ward, "if Kennesaw is given up Atlanta will have the enemy at her doors. And, speaking of Atlanta, now look to the southeast, and you can plainly see the church spires and the smoke from the foundries in Atlanta, twenty miles distant. There is the goal of Sherman's ambition. There is the heart of the Confederacy; and if the Yankees can pierce it, the

Wheeler's cavalry alone had been able to impose upon McPherson, who certainly believed and reported that the intrenchments in his front were held by infantry."—Cox's "Atlanta," pp. 108, 115.

It may be "hardly credible," but Wheeler's cavalry did "impose upon McPherson" nevertheless.

Featherston's division of Loring's corps was extended from the Western & Atlantic Railroad, where its right originally rested, only about a couple of hundred yards east of it, and the rest of the entrenchments of Hood's corps were held by Wheeler's dismounted cavalry.

ALLATOONA PASS, FROM THE SOUTH.

South will then receive her most desperate wound."

"What mountain is that which rises 'solitary and alone' out of the plain to the left of Atlanta?" asked Miss Harper.

"That is Stone Mountain," said Captain Ward, "one of Georgia's curiosities. See, it sits upon the level horizon like a huge cone or helmet."

"Yes, sir," answered the young lady, "I now remember it well."

"And over to the east, beyond Big Kennesaw some five miles or more, is Black Jack Mountain with its several crests. Then look, too, to the north at those high peaks which pierce the horizon. Those are the Allatoona Mountains. If you will examine closely, you can see a depression in the ridge just this side of the mountains. That is Allatoona Pass, an artificial cut over a hundred feet deep, through which the Western & Atlantic railroad emerges from the mountain fastnesses into the open country on this side. All the desperate fighting which we had in the wilderness around New Hope Church was caused by Sherman's flank movement there, which was intended to force us to give up the Allatoona Pass.

"The fighting was the most desperate and bloody which we have had since the campaign opened; but Sherman accomplished his purpose by making the line too long for us to hold with our inferior numbers, and we fell back to Kennesaw.

"The trains, with supplies for the Yankee army, now come through the pass and down to Big

Shanty, which you see over yonder about six miles to the north, but for the present, at least, General Johnston says to them, 'Thus far and no farther.'

"Ah! by the way, Miss Harper," said Captain Ward, "direct the field-glass almost immediately south of us to that house in a grove just by the Dallas road from Marietta, and in the suburbs of Marietta. That is Mr. Kirkpatrick's house, which is General Johnston's headquarters."

"Oh, Captain Ward," said Jack, "the Yankees are down there all along the front of our men, ain't they?"

"Yes, Jack," replied Captain Ward, "it is too true that they are; and they are very close neighbors, too. We had much rather have their room than their company;"—then turning to Miss Harper, he continued:

"Right in front of our line, and not more than some three or four hundred yards distant on an average, the Yankee army is maintaining its death-grapple with ours. Look and see, almost as far as the eye can reach to the southwest, those white dots on the earth show the thousands of tents of the Yankee army. You observe they come in a sort of irregular line up from the south to the west, then make an angle and whiten the fields and forests below us on the north. Occasionally you see hundreds of them apparently grouped together like a town. These are where some divisions are in reserve, instead of being located in line of battle behind regular works. There must be at least ten thousand of them in reach of the eye. Then notice the white specks which are moving in long lines. Those are the Yankee wagon-trains. There are some ambulances for the wounded among them which our boys make them have a good deal of use for. Down yonder to the south in front of Cheatham's and part of Cleburne's lines is Hooker's corps,—'Fighting Joe' Hooker, as the Yankees call him, and it must be admitted that he is a pretty tough fighter; but he has met his match without any question when he faces our redoubtable Tennesseean and the 'Con'ederate Irishman,' as the Yankees call Cleburne. Up at Ringgold, just two days after our defeat at Missionary Ridge, Cleburne gave Hooker a whipping which will go down to history. Hooker, by the way, has the only corps of eastern troops who are in Sherman's army. The rest are western men; and we find the western pioneers are generally harder fighters than eastern shop-clerks; but Hooker partially counteracts that by his personal skill and dash.

"Thence on Hooker's left, and coming up this way, is Palmer's corps. They are good fighters, too, and we have our hands full holding them off; but they have not made such progress as they must naturally desire, even if they have overwhelming numbers. Further up this way, and almost beneath us, is the Fourth Corps, which General Howard commands. He is the one, you know, that Pat Cleburne administered such a terrible drubbing to, over near New Hope Church and

BATTLE OF PICKETT'S MILL. FIRST VOLLEY FROM THE CONFEDERATES.

Pickett's Mill on the 27th of last month, and, by the way, that was northwest of here, to the right of Lost Mountain, which you see rising so prominently over yonder.

"Cleburne was on our right up there, and the Yankees were trying to flank us that evening, and he was ordered to check the movement at all hazards. He took position in the forest on the hillside, and the Yankees came down the opposite hill and up that one in six lines. They marched up the ascending slope until all at once their front line found itself facing Cleburne's men in the open forest. There was not the sign of a breastwork occupied by either. Cleburne made his men hold their fire until the Yankees had come up to within about fifteen paces of them, and then gave the order. Such a destructive volley has scarcely ever been seen in warfare. It is said that out of several hundred men only seven were left standing. The next column came up; but our boys had gotten ready again, and felled nearly every one of them with the second volley. Then they had it hot and heavy for awhile; but the Yankees were utterly routed."

"Then we gave them the worst kind of a beating, didn't we, Captain Ward?" said Jack.

"Yes, Jack," answered Captain Ward, laughing heartily, "we gave them as bad a beating as they ever had;" and, continuing, he said, "Down in front of the mountain, and joining Howard's corps on the left, is Logan's, which extends, fronting us,

WAKING UP THE BATTERIES. 31

to and across the Western & Atlantic Railroad, which crosses Noonday valley on that huge red embankment you see down yonder; and on that little rise which you observe just east of the railroad, the Yankees in his command are constructing a casemated battery which, I fear, will worry us a great deal." *

"What is a casemated battery?" inquired Miss Harper.

"Why, it is one which is covered up. They first make entrenchments and put their cannon in them, and then build a framework of logs above, and on the top they place a timber roof over all these, and on this roof they pile a thick layer of earth, so that a shell from above falling upon it, makes practically

From Report of Gen. P. J. Osterhaus.

* "These sharpshooters had been annoying the artillerists and infantry in my main works considerably. * * * In following up the enemy, however, it was found that he had only fallen back about a mile into a second line of works running along the crest of Kennesaw and on the slope east and west, thus protecting the town of Marietta about three miles in their rear. * * * On the 20th of June, in pursuance to orders received, Col. Williamson's (2nd) Brigade deployed on the crest of the hill to the right of the second division, where he entrenched himself. This position was in the direct front of the rebel batteries placed on the very summit of Big Kennesaw, and exposed to their plunging fire. Between the right of Col. Williamson's line and the (Western & Atlantic) railroad, which here runs through a gap in the mountains, was a considerable interval. * * *

"In order to resist the artillery fire which the enemy constantly kept up from his batteries (as well as musketry fire from the rifle pits on the slope of the mountain) while these lines were being established, I built two casemated batteries for my rifled guns (two 3-inch Rodman and two 20-pound Parrotts."

Gen. Osterhaus adds, regarding the operations of June 23d: "I opened fire from these batteries, and with such precision that the mountain batteries were not only silenced whenever they opened, but were entirely withdrawn June 25th."

This last statement was either an intentional fiction or a careless mistake; for these batteries were not withdrawn until the night of July 2nd, and, in fact, during a part of that day (July 2nd) they maintained, for some two hours or more, a very hot bombardment upon the Federal position below.

no impression. We have either to fire right into a port-hole or our discharge goes for nothing. From this elevation, or from a long distance, a shot will not enter a casemated battery.

"Over on this line to the east of the railroad, fronting Great Kennesaw and extending east of it, is Blair's corps, of McPherson's army, as we understand it. They only arrived at the front and reenforced Sherman's grand army last week. Several days ago they made an impetuous attack upon and captured an entire regiment of our boys. The men on top of the mountain saw the whole thing; but there was no means of signaling them to retreat. *

"And that reminds me, look yonder to the summit of Great Kennesaw, Miss Harper, see that red flag which the man on top of the rock is waving as against the sky. That is our signal flag. That is now being watched through field-glasses from Marietta and from several other points. The man is giving information of the Yankee army's movements as seen from the mountain top.

*"On the 15th we advanced our general lines, intending to attack at any weak point discovered between Kennesaw and Pine Mountain; but Pine Mountain was found to be abandoned, and Johnston had contracted his front somewhat, on a direct line, connecting Kennesaw with Lost Mountain. Thomas and Schofield thereby gained about two miles of most difficult country, and McPherson's left lapped well around the north end of Kennesaw. We captured a good many prisoners, among them a whole infantry regiment, the Fourteenth Alabama, three hundred and twenty strong."—Sherman's Memoirs, Vol. II, page 54.

An uncle of the author was on the mountain top and, through a field-glass, saw the Federals surround this regiment (the Fortieth, instead of the Fourteenth, Alabama) in the forest, and observed them throw down their arms in surrender, and march off to the rear of the Federal position, under guard.

"Oh! how we did wish," said he to the author, "when we saw the Yankees circling through the woods on either side to get behind them, that we had some means of signaling to them from the mountain top, to let them know their danger."

WAKING UP THE BATTERIES. 3

"A few days ago I remember his message was one which brought poignant grief to every man in the army. It was the information that our grand Bishop-General Polk had just been killed on the summit of Pine Mountain. The information was signalled from the station on Pine Mountain to that on Kennesaw, and thence repeated to the other

DEATH OF GENERAL POLK.

stations around here. Ah! that was worse than a killing in battle,—that was a tragedy."

"Yes," exclaimed Miss Harper with a shudder, "that was war's most awful tragedy. May God have mercy upon the hands that did it!"

"After his death," continued Captain Ward, "his remains were brought down to the Hardage house, which you see in that clump of trees yonder to the northwest, and scarcely a half mile from the western end of the mountain. The Burnt Hickory road from Marietta runs right by the house. The body of the noble old man lay in an ambulance under a grand oak tree for a couple of hours before they got everything ready and carried it to Marietta to send to Augusta for burial."

"Yes," said Miss Harper," "I remember coming up from Atlanta on the train several days ago, and the conductor, Mr. Sanford Bell, was telling me that the Bishop's remains were carried down to Atlanta on his train."

"But let us go forward a little," said the captain, "and we can look immediately down the mountain side on the north. Hear that whistle! and look yonder, Miss Harper, toward Big Shanty. See the train of cars coming down the Western & Atlantic Railroad, in the rear of the Yankee lines and toward the mountain. Ah, the rascals! the very same railroad which is our sole dependence for supplies from the south is also their sole means of communication with the north. Where we have it, it is our salvation, and where they have it, it is one of the strongest weapons against us. Their every great movement heretofore has been for the purpose

WAKING UP THE BATTERIES. 35

of breaking it in our rear, and thus paralyzing us; and we could afford to give almost a fourth of our army if we could ruin it in their rear.

"And, by the way, speaking of the railroad reminds me of an achievement by a Yankee engineer several days ago, which, although it chagrined us a good deal at the time, yet, I must confess, appeals more highly to our admiration than to our resentment.

"While a number of us were strengthening our works on the mountain, and otherwise occupying our time as profitably as soldiers on the lookout can, some one called our attention to a locomotive which was coming down from the direction of Big Shanty toward the mountain.

" 'What are they after?' was the general inquiry, 'is it bearing a flag of truce?'

"Through our field-glasses several of us could see the engine as it came at the rate of six or eight miles an hour toward our lines.

"Our soldiers in the breastworks could be observed getting upon the parapets in swarms, and we could imagine the curiosity they felt at seeing the Yankee locomotive coming straight forward, as if its engineer was trying to get away from old Sherman and bring a first-class prize with him as an offering of loyalty to us.

"Suddenly he began to slow down, and within less than a minute the engine stopped, apparently within scarcely a hundred yards in front of our works.

"We then saw her begin to back toward the Yankee lines, after her engineer had first made her give a saucy, shrill whistle which was plainly heard by every man up here.

"The next instant we could see an irregular succession of puffs of smoke breaking forth from all along our breastworks as far as they were within range or sight of her, and a moment afterward the rattling sound of musketry was faintly heard from below.

"'Spying our works, by jingo!' yelled a soldier up here, and another added, 'Ain't that the most audacious trick you ever saw a Yankee play?'

"Another shrill blast of the whistle was heard, as the engine began accelerating her backward motion every instant.

"All at once the boom of a cannon was heard, and we saw the cloud of smoke arising from that high hill on the right of the railroad, which is called Brush Mountain, and a smaller cloud and report right beyond the now flying locomotive told us that a shell had been sent after her by one of our batteries.

"The example was contagious, and from all along the top of the mountain the yell arose, 'Open fire upon the impudent scoundrels, and blow their engine up.'

"Every artilleryman, without needing orders, ran to the guns, and, before a minute had elapsed, one of Guibor's guns banged away and sent a shell after her. But, gracious! the shell missed her fully

WAKING UP THE BATTERIES.   37

three hundred yards. For once in his life Sam Kennard made a bad shot.

"The rest of us followed suit, and the loud reports from Big Kennesaw told that the artillery over there was also after her.

"We could see the smoke from the explosion of our shells and from those on the hills below, but I don't think a single one struck within a hundred yards of the engine. The Yankee escaped, and no doubt was a great hero in his camp,—and deservedly so I must admit, for it was certainly a most daring deed, and one which calls for the applause of all brave men.

"We were naturally a little fretted at the success of the fellow in coming almost into our lines and then giving us the slip, and in the most saucy manner too; but next morning we felt somewhat discomfited when some one told us that a Yankee picket who had been captured, had stated that the engineer and an officer, named Potter, had been sent down toward our lines in the locomotive, by General Sherman's orders, to draw our fire and determine the location of our guns on the mountain and among the hills. He said they were in great glee over the success of the venture.

"You see that was practically the first pass they had made at us since we abandoned the New Hope Church line of defense and assumed this at Kennesaw Mountain, hence the development of the location of our new line was an important matter for them. Their locomotive scheme beat sending forward several thousand men and running them into an ambush, or at least getting them caught between a cross fire from strong works such as we have.

"However, if it was any source of gratification to them, they are welcome to it, for they have not had any success worth bragging about since they have been fighting around Kennesaw, unless we except General Hood's defeat below here yesterday. Hood's rashness and independence of action have, on two or three occasions during the campaign, amounted almost to insubordination. Oh, if Pat Cleburne or Cheatham were only in command of that corps, instead of Hood, we would have every reason to be satisfied! I have heard it intimated that General Hood is quietly intriguing for the command of the army in General Johnston's stead. Woe be to the army, the cause and the country if he succeeds!

"Ah! but look down yonder, Miss Harper, to the right of Big Kennesaw, and close to its base. See that multitude of white spots, some of them moving about in that open field. That is our wagon train. It has been placed, as you see, behind the mountain; but since the Yankees began throwing shells over the summit some two or three days ago they have caused a good deal of confusion down there. General Walthall was speaking of it last night, and laughingly remarked about the shells, which exploded in the air and scattered their fragments promiscuously below, 'Whenever they

WAKING UP THE BATTERIES. 39

fail to hit a man they frighten a mule, consequently the wagon train is in an uproar half the time.'"

"But, oh! what is the matter with those poor fellows who are lying on the ground, while their comrades seem trying to make them comfortable?" asked Miss Harper.

"There has been considerable sickness in our division, as well as others recently," said Captain Ward. "The hot weather, night marches, exposure to heavy rains, loss of sleep and the lack of vegetables, and the consequent diet of bread and bacon only has told on them. I have, in fact for several days, been sick myself, and came on duty this morning for the first time in a week, and, to tell the truth, ought not to have come to-day; but I felt that I ought to be at my post if it were possible. General Johnston is appealing to the people to send us vegetables, and using every means in his power to remedy the evil. Ah! the general public does not appreciate how nobly he watches over his soldiers; but we see it evidenced by a dozen or more proofs every day. Not only does he endeavor to prevent any useless sacrifice of the lives of his men, but he constantly attempts to keep them healthy, and I can safely say that nine-tenths of the men in this army have the most unbounded confidence in their commander. In fact, I have never seen or heard of an army which was so devoted to its leader."

"Oh, Captain, just listen to those cannon firing

over yonder to the west; let's go there and see what's the matter," exclaimed Jack eagerly.

"Yes," said Captain Ward, "there is heavy firing going on below the foot of the mountain, on the west; I have been noticing the sound of the cannon for some minutes; but it is about a mile from here and cannot affect us on the mountain top. But let us go over toward the western slope and watch it. General French, Major Storrs and a number of others have walked that way. And I should like to introduce you to General French and Major Storrs. They are both such perfect gentlemen, as well as splendid commanders."

"Oh! Captain, is it safe to go?" asked Miss Harper. "Had we better do so?"

"There is no danger at all up here, Miss Harper," he answered, "the fighting is on the hills about six hundred feet below us, and fully a mile away from the foot of the mountain."

They walked down the crest, and at one point behind Guibor's battery, the captain remarked:

"Here was where Lieutenant McBride was killed by a Yankee cannon shot last Saturday. He was at the time in command of this battery, Captain Guibor being absent, as he still is, from sickness."

"General Johnston sent orders for the batteries on Kennesaw Mountain to open actively on the enemy and draw their fire, and thus develop their position and the number of their pieces of artillery.

"This we did, and we soon had a considerable bombardment directed against us from along their

WAKING UP THE BATTERIES.   41

line. In the midst of this, Major Storrs got upon a large rock, which I will show you to the west of us, to count their guns. He was thus occupied for about a half hour, and, from counting them over carefully several times, found that we were under fire from one hundred and forty cannon. One of their missiles struck McBride and killed him. Poor fellow! he was a splendid officer and a most noble gentleman. He was one who was always ready for any emergency; but his is now the soldier's last sleep: he has fought his last fight and the reveille will awake him no more. But to change the subject a minute," added the captain, "here is my battery near the end of the peak. I have four Napoleons, as they are called. You see them here behind the parapets of rock which we have piled up on the otherwise almost naked surface of granite; and I suppose you have, within the past three days, seen the smoke of our guns even from the windows of your home in Marietta."

They soon reached the western end of the peak, and stood upon an immense bald, rocky formation which was its extreme point. From here the descent was very steep, and there was an unobstructed view for miles to the west and south. General French and Major Storrs were standing here with General Cockrell and General Ector, the latter of whom had just returned from a visit to General Johnston's headquarters; and, as Captain Ward and his party came up, General French who stood facing her, bowed very politely to the young lady, and Captain Ward immediately introduced her to the three officers.

General French remarked, "This reminds me of a visit of one of the Graces to Olympus, the home of the thunder-clouds."

"Yes," said Miss Harper, "and since I have gotten up here, I have thought for twenty times or more that the Grace had better have staid at home and left Mars alone to associate with Jupiter."

"Oh, well," said General French, with a laugh, "there have been things done which were more imprudent than this."

"And you can say another thing, Miss Harper," said General Cockrell, "and that is that very few ladies in Georgia have looked down upon a battle, as you are now doing."

"And," said General Ector, "if our boys down yonder only knew how fair a face was directed toward them from up here almost among the clouds, they would fight as they have hardly ever fought before. You are observing what very few ladies have ever had equal chances of seeing."

"Yes," added Major Storrs, "there are very few ladies who have witnessed so fierce a bombardment from opposing batteries without being in any danger."

"Here we are up on the eagle's perch," said Captain Ward, "and we can, without fear, glance downward upon the dangers of those who are hundreds of feet below us."

"But," said Miss Harper, as she looked back at

WAKING UP THE BATTERIES.   43

one of Captain Ward's pieces of artillery, "we are, as General French said a minute or so ago, on Georgia's Olympus whence the thunderbolts dart."

"Well," answered Captain Ward, "I hope the Yankees will think they are worse than thunderbolts by the time I get an opportunity to open upon them."

"But, look, Miss Harper," said General French, "see, down to the west of us, the dense clouds of smoke which are rising from our lines and those of the Yankees. There you will notice those quick puffs which burst forth as from the earth. The sound is like near thunder. The Yankees have over thirty pieces of artillery concentrated against a portion of our lines. Now look through this glass, and you can see strong columns of the enemy advancing under cover of that heavy bombardment, and they are driving in our skirmishers. Those little whiffs of smoke which from up here appear no larger than the puff from a cigar, are the discharges from our skirmish line. There, they come in pretty regular array. You see the heavy work which is being done by our batteries. Those are on our main line, and the Yankees had as well give up any attempt against that." *

---

* "JUNE 23.—In accordance with request of General Thomas I tried an intrenched height in front of General Newton's and Stanley's position, it being doubted whether or not this was a position of the enemy's main line. I opened upon it a concentrated artillery fire from as many guns as I could bring to bear, and immediately afterwards advanced a strong skirmish line, which drove the enemy within his works and developed a heavy artillery and musketry fire. By this operation I advanced our lines, particularly on the extreme right, to very close proximity to the rebel works. These proved to be his main lines, covered by troublesome abatis and other entanglements."—Gen. O. O. Howard's Report of Operations of the Fourth Army Corps.

They gazed intently at the exciting melee in the woods far below them, the scene being somewhat obscured, however, by the smoke, and then, as the little force of Confederates was seen retreating in groups, firing as they fled before the storm of shells and the heavy infantry lines, Miss Harper exclaimed:

"Oh! the sound of the guns is terrible. Do you really think our soldiers will be able to hold our position? See how strong the Yankee line is, compared with ours."

"Yes, but if you were down there and could see our men, you would not have any fear that the Yankee column which is now moving against it, would be able to break it," answered General French.

They stood for nearly a quarter of an hour longer, observing the fight which was going on. This was principally, however, an artillery duel, with the exception that the Federals had moved forward under cover of the fire of about thirty pieces of artillery and had somewhat advanced their position toward the Confederate main works.

"Captain Ward, what is that man doing?" asked Jack, pointing to a soldier who was sitting on a large rock with a pencil and a sheet of paper, intently surveying the panorama below, and leisurely sketching it.

"Ah!" answered the captain, "he is drawing a picture of the fight, Jack. Some of our soldiers are apt artists."

WAKING UP THE BATTERIES. 45

"Yes," said the soldier with a smile, "but it's a safe disciple of art I am this time, as I am not under fire, but securely perched above the fire. '*Tomada en globo*' (taken from a balloon) the Spaniards say of some panoramic pictures taken mid-air by venturesome photographers; but I am beating them, for I have a firmer foundation to rest my easel on."

"Let me see," said Miss Harper, leaning over and surveying his sketch, "upon my word, you have made such a true picture. There is Lost Mountain on the horizon, then the undulating hills, and below us is the open field at the end of the mountain, and the dotted lines showing the advancing columns of soldiers and the little clouds of smoke. There is everything, except the sound."

"Thank you kindly, Miss," answered the soldier with a bow, "I will always be proud of the compliment."

General French then remarked, "Well, I think that we have seen the termination of to-day's fight. The enemy have no idea of an assault at present upon our line, and this is merely the cover to a partial forward movement."

Captain Ward exclaimed, "Yes, that's so. Now Miss Harper, let us go back to the middle of the peak, and see how matters are getting along there. I wish to point out one or two other objects of interest to you."

With a polite bow to General French and the

other officers, Captain Ward and his party then left them.

"Captain Ward, is that man waving his flag so as to show the old Yankees that we have still got the mountain and they can't take it away from us?" asked Jack, as they observed an officer on top of a high rock near the western end of the mountain and just where it began sloping down toward the north.

"No, Jack, not exactly that," answered the captain; "but he is on observation here, and is signaling to our men on the front side of Big Kennesaw, and to the observation post west of Marietta, and giving them the news of the progress and result of the fight down below us. I am glad it is favorable news to-day.

"That is what we call 'Observation Rock.' From it Major Storrs counted the Yankee guns, as I was saying a while ago; and every day the officer on observation duty on this end of the mountain takes his position upon it, and from there can see everything to the north and west, and also to the south. You could, if you were upon it, look over the backbone of the mountain where we are, and trace our line, with a field-glass, clear down to the hill where General Cheatham's division rests, nearly three miles to the south, besides noticing the general level of the country for miles beyond."

"What a queer rock it is!" said Jack, "you can look under it and see the hills and fields and the Yankee tents in front of the mountain."

WAKING UP THE BATTERIES. 47

"Yes," answered the captain, "the tempests of a great many ages have washed the under side of it until it seems to rest upon the mountain top as if

OBSERVATION ROCK.

it was not there originally, but had been thrown up here by some great giant's hand."

"Whoopee!" exclaimed Jack with some enthusiasm, "Jack, the giant-killer, would have had a hard time killing him, wouldn't he?"

"I should think he would have," replied Captain Ward with a smile; "but let us go."

"This is your battery, I believe you said a few minutes ago, did you not, Captain Ward?" asked the young lady, as they were passing the guns near the western end of the crest.

"Yes, these are mine,—four Napoleons," replied the captain, "and just beyond me to the east are three Napoleon guns of Guibor's Missouri battery. Their other gun was damaged by a Yankee shot, and has been sent to Marietta for repairs. These Missourians are magnificent fighters, and they are adepts in handling this battery.

"Then, on their right, and near the northeastern end of Little Kennesaw, is a section, or two guns, of Hoskins' Mississippi battery. They have fine pieces, and they deserve them. There are four brothers named Hoskins in this battery, one of whom, Captain Jim Hoskins, commands it. They are splendid soldiers, and theirs is very justly considered one of our crack batteries. The other guns of this battery are down the western slope of the mountain, or rather of the hill below us which is really the continuation of the mountain."

CHAPTER III.

They soon reached the eastern end of the ridge and stood behind a long rock, over which they could look through a glass at the prospect below.

"What are those men after, who are going down the mountain side with their guns?" inquired Miss Harper.

"They are sharpshooters, who intend trying to pick off some of the men in that group in the field down in front of us," replied Captain Ward. "I thought they had gone down some minutes ago; but they seem to have been delayed."

"They were just getting ready," said a private standing by, "but now they're going to take a crack at the Yankees."

"Oh, my! then let us get away from here. It would be terrible to witness the death of any person, even if an enemy," exclaimed the young lady, with a shudder.

"No, Sis, let's see if they hit 'em," said Jack.

"Oh, no indeed, let us at least get out of sight until this dreadful scene is over. I cannot remain longer," said his sister.

"Well then, if you will go," answered the captain, "there is a large rock back yonder, behind which you can both find shelter from even the severest bombardment. Just take them down there, Minon, till we see what comes of this. If the Yankees don't get after Partridge, they can come back here within half an hour, and we will show them, in detail, war's most imposing panorama below us. It is well worth staying to see."

"I think we had better return home!" replied Miss Harper.

"No, Sis, you go back behind the rock, and I will stay with Captain Ward," said Jack.

"Jack," said the captain, "you are now one of my soldiers; I detail you to protect your sister. Go back with her,—those are my orders."

"All right, captain," was the reply, "but can't I come back after a while?"

"You must not come till I tell you to do so," said the captain.

Miss Mary smiled at the droll scene, and the captain's eye twinkled, while Jack with childish lack of guile took it all in sober earnestness.

Minon then took the two behind the gigantic rock, and, spreading a blanket on the grass, exclaimed, "Remain here, Miss Harper, and Jack, till I return. You are in no danger here."

"All right; but if any trouble comes, you will see us safely home at once," answered the young lady.

"Certainly, I will take care of you," exclaimed Minon, and then with a bow hastened back to his post at the guns.

WAKING UP THE BATTERIES.   51

Soon the sharp crack of a rifle rang out from amid the cliffs.

About a minute later two others were heard.

The venturesome Federals, however, were not observed as showing any concern.

"Wait till you hear from Partridge," exclaimed Captain Ward to Captain Hoskins, who had expressed a fear that they had not gotten the range; "he's sheltered behind that big crag to the right."

He had hardly spoken before "bang!" went Partridge's gun.

"Ho! ho!" exclaimed Col. Young, who, like Captain Ward, was watching the scene through a field glass, "he's brought down the game."

"Yes," added Captain Ward, "one of them has fallen from his horse, and there is quite a flutter among the rest. They are getting back into the woods in a hurry. But see that fellow galloping away toward the battery near the railroad this side of Noonday Creek."

Another report of a sharpshooter's rifle interrupted, and Captain Ward added:

"A first rate shot; he's tumbled him out of the saddle. I won't have to return that battery's compliments until they send another messenger of evil tidings to it."

"That was Porter's shot. He winged the bird as it flew," said Lieutenant Murphy, of Guibor's battery, who was down the slope watching the riflemen.

"Confound this atmosphere," exclaimed an artilleryman, "it's so heavy that the smoke from those Enfield rifles hangs around the crags like cotton. The Yankees can see it with their glasses, and they will get the range of our Partridge nest, and shell the boys behind cover."

"That's so, Tom," said Colonel Young, "and I see two horsemen hurrying toward the battery."

Just then Generals French and Cockrell and Colonel Barry joined the group in front of the parapet, and the former asked, "Are the boys interfering with the curiosity seekers?"

"Yes, General," replied Colonel Young, "they have only a minute ago scattered a party who were in the edge of that field down yonder. They shot down two of them."

Three reports rang out in quick succession, and Colonel Barry remarked, "The music from the smaller instruments is beginning."

"Yes, but wait a few minutes," said Captain Ward, "and you will hear the big bass drum. That battery down in front is going to open, if I mistake not."

"Yes," added Captain Hoskins, "and as there is no telling how far this will spread, I'll hurry down to my two guns on the hill," and walked rapidly toward the west.

A couple of minutes passed, during which the parapets were lined with officers and soldiers, whose attention had been attracted by the rifle shots.

Suddenly a volume of white smoke burst forth

WAKING UP THE BATTERIES. 53

from the top of the hill far below, and then the sullen boom of a cannon woke the air.

"That's so, look out for it!" exclaimed Colonel Barry, and a second later a puff of smoke arose from the forest growth about a hundred yards below, to the right, and the sharp report of an exploding shell rang out.

"Pretty good," said General Cockrell, "Hurrah for that gunner! he's come very near landing his very first charge in the midst of the boys."

A derisive yell arose from the sharpshooters, and several other shots were fired by them.

About a minute later two other guns in the Federal battery opened upon them; but these fired wide of the mark, the shells falling fully two hundred yards from the sharpshooters' nest.

Then the crack of a rifle succeeded, and officers and men alike burst into a roar of laughter.

"That's a magnificent duel," exclaimed Major Storrs, "a bunch of riflemen and a battery, over a half a mile apart, firing at each other."

"It may be well if it is confined to them;" remarked General French, "but it is best to be prepared to reciprocate any gratuitous favors which those gunners may dispense for our benefit up here. Major, hadn't you better arrange for Captain Ward and Lieutenant Harris to silence that battery if it gets too familiar?"

"Yes, General, Captain Ward has promised already to stand by the boys if they get into trouble," answered Major Storrs; and then, turning to

Captain Ward, he remarked, "Captain, suppose you get ready for that fellow if he fires again."

"All right, Major," said Captain Ward, "I'll try to fix him so that he won't send any more than one 'R. S. V. P.' missive to us," then turning to E. R. Matthews, who carried the battery flag, he remarked, "Matthews, fasten the colors to that stump of a sapling in front of the parapet. We want it in front of our guns, and in full view of the enemy for miles around."

Just as he started toward one of the guns in his battery, which was about a hundred yards west from where they were standing, and had called three of his men to join him, three almost simultaneous puffs of smoke arose from the Federal battery; and the reports had scarcely reached the ears of those on the mountain top before two shells exploded among the crags near the sharpshooters' den, and a third buried itself in the ground about thirty yards below General French and his party, and exploded, scattering earth, rocks and fragments on every side.

"Well, gentlemen, you have received the invitation to the ball; I think you should accept it, and lead those chaps as lively a dance as 'old Dan Tucker,'" said General French to Major Storrs and the artillery captains. "We haven't a very great amount of artillery ammunition; but we had better fire a few rounds and impress them with the fact that we are on the vigorous defensive."

WAKING UP THE BATTERIES.　　55

"Yes," said the major, "let the men come to their posts and prepare for action."

A general hurrah followed, and the artillerymen hurried to their guns all along the line.

"Ah, banner of beauty!" exclaimed the captain, pausing a moment and gazing at the flag of the Confederacy, as it fluttered in the breeze above his battery, with its blue cross and bright stars amid the square of red in the upper left hand corner and the snowy whiteness of the balance of it. "What nation," he added, "ever boasted a flag so chaste and elegant? How much prettier it is than the old stars and stripes! Whenever I look quietly at it, I find myself wishing that I were a Byron or a Scott, so that I might express in words the real poetry with which it lights up my soul. Yes, whether I look at the national flag or its child, the battle flag, I feel like calling down the benison of holy Heaven upon it and all who are true to it. May a gracious God bless the South and the flag of her love!"

"Yes," said Major Storrs, "that's the prettiest banner I ever beheld, and it is typical of our glorious Southland. Long may it wave, and long may she stand, the abode of liberty and happiness."

"Those are all sentiments that each of us indorses," added Colonel Barry.

General French, Major Storrs and Colonels Young and Barry joined Captain Ward, who had taken personal charge of one of the pieces.

"Let me cut that fuse, Tom," said the captain to

one of the men who had brought forward a shell. "I think a three seconds' length will just about get the range of that battery. Now, elevate her barely a span, boys: there, that's too much,—lower her, ah! now you've got it; now turn her a little to the left,—ha! she's right at last. Now, Cruse," said he, addressing his first lieutenant, who was very fleshy, and wore eye-glasses, "pull off your own eyes and try this field glass, and let me know just where my shell goes."

Nearly half a minute succeeded, then, as Captain Ward himself pulled the lanyard, a cloud of smoke shot out, enveloping everything for yards around, and a deafening roar shook the mountain top and reverberated like thunder through the air far toward the Etowah Valley and the Allatoona Mountains.

"A good shot, Captain Ward, you can't do that again," exclaimed General French, "you landed your shell right in the midst of that Yankee battery; and that's a caisson that's exploded."

"Yes," laughed Cruse, "when I was cashier in a bank I never handled money and made it fit the calculations any closer than you did that gun."

A wild yell of applause arose from the artillerymen and the spectators.

"Well, I'm prepared to admit," said Captain Ward, "that that was a fortunate accident, and that I couldn't do it again in twenty shots."

"Golly, Mass John, dat was a noble shot!" exclaimed Woodson, Captain Ward's negro cook,

WAKING UP THE BATTERIES. 57

"ef you giv' 'em anudder one like dat dey'll want to git back ahind de Oostanauley for sho'. Sock it to 'em agin."

"Yes, drat 'em," added Daily, General French's cook, "dey broke my pans yestiddy wid one o' dar splodin' bumshells, an' I can't [cook good till I git some more. Smash 'em good wid de nex' shot." *

"Now, let them have it again, boys," called Major Storrs, "that was a fine beginning; let the good work go on."

"Hurrah for Joe Johnston and the Southern Confederacy!" shouted the gunners, and, some three or four minutes later, from Guibor's and Ward's batteries three thunderous reports in quick succession rang out from Kennesaw's crest, and a few seconds afterward three puffs of smoke near the Federal battery and three explosions, "faint from farther distance borne," told that payment in their own coin had been tendered the enemy.

An answer came back within a couple of minutes in a shell from the Federal battery, which struck about half way up the mountain side and exploded.

"Ah! they're demoralized by your shot, Captain Ward," said General Cockrell, "that was rather wild."

* "Thousands of their Parrott shells pass high over the mountain, and exploding at a great elevation, the after part of the shell is arrested in its flight, and falling perpendicularly, comes into camp, and they have injured our tents. Last night I heard a peculiar "thug" on my tent, and a rattle of tin pans, and this morning my negro boy cook put his head into my tent and said: "See here, Master Sam, them, 'fernal Yanks done shot my pans last night. What am I going to do 'bout it?" A rifle ball coming over the mountain, had fallen from a great height, and, perforating the pans, had entered the ground.—From Gen. French's Diary during June, 1864.

A rifle shot was now heard from Partridge's perch, and a general laugh again arose.

"Hurrah for the sharpshooters!" said Colonel Samuels, "they're entitled to a part in this fight."

Just at that moment from the hill behind the Western & Atlantic railroad, on the other side of Noonday Creek, a cloud of smoke arose, and an angry "boom!" shook the air.

"Another Richmond in the field!" exclaimed Major Storrs. "They are not waiting to finish the casemating of that battery of Parrotts and Rodmans before trying to make it as offensive as possible to us."

He had not ceased speaking ere the scream of a shell was heard above their heads, and, before the two darkey cooks had finished dodging toward the ground, the explosion was heard behind them, and, on looking around, the curling smoke amid the forest, some seven hundred yards south of the mountain top, showed how far the deadly missile had sped.

"That was a bad one," said Colonel Samuels.

"Regular pizen," exclaimed a soldier, "if that fellow don't cool off, we'll have to rub a wet sponge over his face."

"Take care, Daily!" shouted a private who had seen the two darkeys hugging the ground with a desperate clutch, "them thar things with shucks to the'r tails are after you and Woodson. Thar's no mark for a Yankee shell like a nigger."

"God almighty! boss, don't make fun of us now,"

WAKING UP THE BATTERIES. 59

whispered Woodson, "I'd give a thousand dollars if I had never heard tell of a Yankee."

A roar of laughter ensued from the soldiers who heard this last remark, and Pat Quin, one of the crack shots of Guibor's battery, exclaimed, "Well now, I don't know how much that offer is worth, begorra, till you tell me whether you mean Confederate money, Yankee greenbacks or the world's specie."

"All of 'em, boss, an' copper too," answered Woodson, as he raised his head with a grin on his face, which reminded every one of the little boy in the graveyard who began whistling to keep his courage up.

"Boom! boom!" again went Captain Ward's guns, and another shell struck near the first Federal battery. Its companion, however, exploded in the air only about a hundred feet from the muzzle, and almost over the infantry line, which ran just below the summit.

"There was bad powder in that one," said the captain, "that's one of our difficulties."

Another cloud of smoke and another report arose from the battery across the railroad, and a Parrott shell struck the side of the mountain about a hundred feet below the crest.

"That means that we are considered as entitled to respectful attention," said Major Storrs; "and that we reciprocate all courtesies in kind," he added, as another of Guibor's guns, aimed by Lieutenant Sam Kennard, went off, waking all the echoes of the mountain, and landing a shell close to the nearest Federal battery.

Hardly a minute afterwards a sound, now somewhat familiar, was heard to the west, and the inevitable white smoke told that the warlike contagion was spreading.

The next instant another shell flew, hissing like a snake, over the mountain, and, falling to the ground a half mile southward, exploded.

"Aha!" exclaimed General Cockrell, "that battery of twenty-pounder Parrott guns over behind the Hardage house has concluded to join the chorus. I'll go down and have Captain Hoskins to take it under his special charge."

"Yes, gentlemen," said General French, "you had better prepare for a lively time. Everybody to his post, and be ready to open all the batteries."

"Hurrah! hurrah! hurrah!" came from several of the officers, and then a wild "rebel yell" ran down the whole line, as the men left their exposed position on the north side of the mountain and went to their places behind the parapets.

It was well they did, for the last man had just about gotten within shelter when from a hill east of the Lattimer place a couple of guns were fired, and a shell struck the cliff above Cockrell's works and exploded, scattering the rocks and fragments in fifty directions. The other buried itself in the earth just a few feet below and in front of Captain Ward's battery, and went off, enveloping the para-

WAKING UP THE BATTERIES. 61

pet in smoke, and throwing mud, etc., on every side.

Almost co-ordinately the battery which had begun the racket, sent another shell over the mountain, and its explosion a few hundred yards beyond told everybody to "lie low."

Ward's and Guibor's batteries now opened in a grand chorus, and Hoskins' two guns on the right took up the refrain, amid the cheers of the soldiery, till the mountain was crowned with uproar.

This found its echo on the hills on either side of the railroad, as the bursting shells whitened the atmosphere with thick smoke, and woke the forest around the Federal guns and gunners who had brought on the affray.

But then almost simultaneously a half dozen batteries on the north and northwest, on either side of Noonday creek, joined their thunders with those of their comrades of tumult, and a shower of exploding shells and whirring solid shot fell below or flew screaming over the parapets on the mountain top. *

"They must do better than that," said Major Storrs, "or it will be a pure waste of the raw material by the Yankee gunners. Now, gentlemen, show them how to fire. Give it to them like we did last Monday! Hurrah for the batteries on Kennesaw!"

---

* JUNE 23 —At 10 a. m., when all was quiet on the mountain, the enemy commenced a rapid artillery fire from guns put in position during the night, and concentrated it on our guns on the mountain. Yesterday we had it all our own way—to-day they are repaying us and the cannonade is "fast and furious."—From Gen. French's Diary during June, 1864.

"And hurrah for the sharpshooters!" yelled Partridge from the crags below.

SHARPSHOOTERS.

"Yes, hurrah for the sharpshooters!" said Major Storrs good-humoredly, "even if they do get us into trouble occasionally."

"Hurrah for Guibor's guns!" exclaimed Lieutenant Harris, "beat that if you can."

"They'll have to try a good many times before they do it, lieutenant," said Colonel Young, who

WAKING UP THE BATTERIES. 63

was looking through his field glass in the direction of Harris' shot. "You dropped that shell right into the midst of a column of Yankee cavalry, and I think you must have killed or wounded at least a dozen or so of them. Lord! how the rest are scattering. To say it's a stampede hardly describes it. Every fellow's going in a different direction, and every fellow seems trying to outrun a shell which he thinks, is after him particularly. Ha, ha, ha! I think at least twenty have been thrown, and are sprawling on the ground, and the horses,—well, nobody can catch them now. Your single shell has routed them as badly as Wheeler did Garrard* and his cavalry several days ago."

"Ha, ha, ha, ha," went down the entire line.

* "On the 20th the most considerable cavalry affair of the campaign occurred on our right. The Confederate cavalry on that flank, being attacked by that under General Garrard's command, repulsed the assailants, whom, as they were retiring, Wheeler charged with about a thousand men, and routed, capturing a hundred men and horses, and two standards. Fifty of the enemy's dead were counted on the field. The Confederate loss was fifteen killed and fifty wounded."—Johnston's Narrative, page 339.

CHAPTER IV.

"Minon," said Captain Ward, "you had better go back and tell Miss Harper and her little brother to stay closely behind that rock. They are safer there now than they would be descending the mountain; for some one of those shells which are flying over the crest might explode, and strike them with a fragment. Let them remain sheltered where they are."

The young sergeant hurried back, and found her in a state of much apprehension; but she took in the situation and readily consented to comply with Captain Ward's suggestion.

"But, oh! I do wish we had not come!" she exclaimed, "this was so foolish a trip."

"No, I am glad we came, Mr. Minon; ask Captain Ward to please let me go out and see it," said Jack in a tone of great eagerness.

"No, Jack, Captain Ward orders you to stay here and protect your sister," answered Minon, "and now I must hurry back," he added, bowing to Miss Harper.

"God shield you from all harm!" she replied clasping her hands.

WAKING UP THE BATTERIES. 65

"Minon, where are Miss Harper and her little brother who were with you about a half hour ago?" asked General French who saw him as he returned.

"They are back yonder behind the large rock, General," the young sergeant replied.

"The mischief, they are!" exclaimed the general, "why what made you keep them here?—however, there's no need to discuss that now. Do you go at once and have some men to take those planks and poles which are around that ammunition chest, and lean against the rock behind them, so as to protect them as much as possible from the explosion of shells. I think we are going to have a good many of them screaming around here within a few minutes, and it won't do for them to attempt now to go back to Marietta till things quiet down again."

With a tip of his hat Minon hurried off to carry out the general's orders.

Miss Harper was greatly agitated by these extraordinary preparations for her safety, and again exclaimed, "What a foolish trip this was!"

Jack, however, as usual, was equal to the occasion, and piped out, "Oh, don't be afraid, Sis; I'll stay here with you."

Boom! boom! boom! went the batteries on Kennesaw, and now the patches of smoke above the plain showed that the Confederates had turned their attention to several of the Federal challengers.

"See," said Major Storrs, who had raised his field glass for a minute to watch the effect of the fire from his guns, "the inhabitants of the temporary city in the woods below us will find this rain somewhat worse for them than that other kind they had last night. Their sharpshooters whom I see at their customary devilment down yonder will probably seek shelter within a few minutes and some of their artillerymen may have occasion to wish that they had more casemates."*

But over hill and forest from beyond the slopes lining Nonday valley east of the railroad, to and beyond the Wallace house on the far west, thence along the line running southward, a chain of rising clouds of smoke, and angry reports, told that battery after battery had opened upon the mountain. The most practical evidence to the Confederates, however, of this fact, was the tempest of Parrott shells, solid shot, and other deadly missiles which came crashing against the crags or flew hurtling through the air above them.* The shout of the war god had been heard!

"Withdraw the infantry from the breastworks in front, Colonel Barry," said General French; "I think this will be merely a bombardment from the batteries, and our men should not be needlessly exposed."

"Yes, sir," answered Colonel Barry, and then sent orders for Sears' brigade to defile behind the breastworks toward the ravine on the east, so as to be sheltered by the mountain from the shells.

* Kennesaw Mountain is no longer a place of resort, owing to the large number of shells hourly sent there by the enemy.
The view from there during the forenoon was obstructed by a heavy fog, hanging like a pall over the valley beneath, and a large glass failed to pierce it and locate the position of the enemy.—Augusta Constitutionalist, June 23, 1864.

WAKING UP THE BATTERIES. 67

The command was obeyed in perfect order, and within a few minutes there was no exposure to the Federal fire, except that of artillerymen who were handling the batteries.

These had hurried to their guns from one end of the summit to the other, and the enthusiastic energy with which they went at their work, was attested by the continuous explosions which appeared to almost shake the mountain, and the dense volumes of white smoke which, like a storm cloud, enveloped its towering crest.

This was plainly visible in Atlanta, twenty miles distant, to hundreds of people who thronged the hill at the western end of Alabama street, or climbed to the tops of buildings, or swarmed like bees on the Broad street bridge, and gazed with breathless interest at the smoking mountain, and strained their ears to catch the booming sounds which, like distant thunder, kept shaking the air; while from the streets and windows of Marietta, which were filled by hundreds of citizens and soldiers, it is said to have presented a scene of grandeur, whose only parallel might be found in a volcanic eruption.* The smoke rising in tremendous columns high above the crest, the thunderous reports from the Confederate batteries, and the explosions, over toward the

---

* "From this time, June 20, until the evening of the 26th, our position was not materially changed. Under direct fire from the rebel skirmishers, no man could expose himself without being a mark for their bullets. They kept our men closely confined to their trenches, and the only variety they had was the constant succession of artillery duels between our batteries and those on the mountain top, which might be looked for at any time of the day or night; at times these assumed a degree of magnificence."
—From Report of Major General A. Baird.

town, of the Federal shells, which had darted through the war clouds, all told a tale of awe and magnificence.

But if it was a magnificent spectacle to those who beheld it from their homes in Marietta, hardly two miles distant, it was one where tumult and danger walked hand in hand with grandeur, in the eyes of the men who stood behind the parapets and amid the crags on the crest of Kennesaw Mountain.

The thick, sulphurous smoke from their own pieces enveloped everything around them in obscurity. This was lit up in quick succession by the flash of fire which burst forth with every discharge and, like lightning among the clouds, shot its glare for the instant all around.

But the terrific majesty of the scene was exhibited in the explosion of the Federal shells, and the crashing of solid shot, above and amid the crags and rocky parapets behind which the Confederate guns were posted on the crown of the mountain.

From one hundred and forty guns on the surrounding hills and forests Sherman's commanders had concentrated their fire upon the crest of Little Kennesaw.*

* "There emphatically was such a bombardment repeatedly. I do not know exactly upon how many days they opened with at least 140 guns, with their aim actually directed to the crests of Big and Little Kennesaw; but do not think it would be too much to say that this occurred on at least ten separate days, and sometimes we would receive two or three bombardments on one day.

"Sometimes when I would fire a few rounds on some exposed body of the enemy, my nine guns would receive the concentrated fire of shot and shell from 140 guns or more, until a thousand or fifteen hundred projectiles had been thrown at us. The fire was absolutely terrific."—From letter written by Major Geo. S. Storrs to the author.

WAKING UP THE BATTERIES. 69

For scores of yards downward the ground was torn up, and the cliffs were scarred. Hundreds of the messengers of wrath flew screaming over the heads of Major Storrs' cannoniers, and exploded far above or in the forests in the valley behind them. Others darted crashing through the trees on the summit, scattering the branches on every side, and bursting into myriad pieces, with spiteful flashes of fire and clouds of stifling smoke which hung like a pall of horror above the mountain. Yet others dashed against the tremendous bowlders on the summit, or struck the huge rocks which had been, with patient labor, piled before the guns as a parapet, and, exploding, spread destruction on every side.

Here a poor fellow in Ward's battery had his head blown off, and beside him were two others wounded by a bursting shell. A solid shot tore off the arm of a man in Guibor's battery, while Hoskins' battery had two wounded within a few minutes.

Henry O'Hara, of this battery, was with one of the two guns which were on the summit of the mountain. He had gone to the ammunition chest, and was bringing forward three charges of fixed ammunition* when a shell burst so close to him as

---

* The Confederates, while on the summit of Kennesaw Mountain, protected their artillery ammunition by digging holes in the ground some thirty or forty feet behind the guns, and burying the chests therein. Covering them with logs cut from the timber on and near the summit of the mountain, they thus secured very fair protection. Only one chest was thus provided for the supply of each gun. The infantry brought the current supply up by hand as it was needed, and deposited it in the chests. From two to four

to explode the nine pounds of powder in his arms. A terrific sheet of fire and smoke enveloped him, and, as he fell backward, some one exclaimed, "My God! it's burnt him up!"

ASSISTING A COMRADE.

His comrades rushed forward, seized him, and men were specially detailed from the infantry to bring the supply required for each gun.

On the hill beyond the western end of Little Kenncsaw, which was occupied by General Cockrell's brigade, Captain Jas. A. Hoskins was in charge of his two guns, which were posted there, and also the guns of Lumsden's Alabama battery. One day, subsequent to that whose events are herein chronicled, three of Lumsden's chests were blown up by the Federal fire. They were within thirty feet of each other, and the result of the explosion, it is quite needless to say, was disastrous to the battery, and the fact of the occurrence, in spite of all the precautions to prevent it, furnishes one of the best evidences of the terrific nature of the Federal bombardment.

WAKING UP THE BATTERIES. 71

carried him to the rear. His clothes were badly burnt and his body, face and limbs blackened by the powder; but, as he stoutly asserted, he was "not done for yet," and within a few weeks was back on duty.

"He was Irish," as some of the boys s id, "and you couldn't expect such a small matter as that to knock him out."

But in the meanwhile with courage which might have excited the envy of Titans, the Confederates stood to their guns, and poured back a shower of shot and shell among the Federals on the hills below. The roar of their batteries from amid the clouds of smoke which enveloped the mountain top found its counterpart in the explosion of shells which darted like thunderbolts among the Federal camps and into the midst of the batteries which were hurling storms of destruction against them.

Just at this period, General French, who was talking with Major Storrs and Col. Barry, noticed, coming toward them, the sergeant who had been sent down to General Sears' headquarters.

"Well, you've got back, I see," he remarked.

"Yes, sir, I delivered your message to General Sears," answered the sergeant.

"And what did he say?" asked the general.

With a smile, after a slight pause, the sergeant answered:

"He says to me, 'Go back and tell General French I'm not a mountain billy-goat to be jumping from cliff to cliff.'"

A roar of laughter followed from the party, after which General French remarked:

"If that message had have come from a lieutenant or a private, it would have been called insubordination; but all we'll say about it now is that Sears is sick, and consequently irritable."

Suddenly a wild, thrilling yell arose from the infantry in the ravine. It was taken up by those who were sheltered on the southern slope behind the batteries; and Lieutenant Harris, peering through the battle smoke in that direction, swung his hat above his head and shouted: "The big guns on Big Kennesaw have joined us. Now, boys, fire fast, and let the Yankees have a regular Confederate concert."

"Yes," added Major Storrs, "don't reduce a cartridge. Give them all the guns will stand."

Their enthusiasm was well founded, for, like successive claps of thunder, the big siege guns on the crest of Big Kennesaw* had opened upon the Federals; and already dense clouds of smoke were hanging around it on every side.

Some of the Confederates, who had taken position behind the crags and amid the thick forest and undergrowth on the east side of the ravine which separates the two summits of Kennesaw, said that

---

*"You may make the necessary orders and be prepared for rapid action to-morrow. So dispose matters that the big guns of Kennesaw will do you as little mischief as possible."—Dispatch from Gen. Sherman to Gen. McPherson, June 22, 1864.

We have some very heavy guns on Kennesaw Mountain which annoy the enemy very much, and they keep out of our reach as much as possible.—Augusta Constitutionalist, June 26, 1864.

WAKING UP THE BATTERIES. 73

the scene was one where the terrible grandeur of war defied all powers of description.

Beginning east of Brush Mountain, and extending in an irregular line across the railroad westward to the neighborhood of the Lattimer house, and thence curving southwestward till they disappeared from view behind Little Kennesaw, dense clouds of smoke rose in quick succession from scores and scores of guns in the Federal batteries. From two or three casemated batteries toward the west these sudden puffs reminded one of the fire from gunboats. There was but little air stirring, consequently an almost continuous chain of fog seemed hovering above the hills and valleys north and west of the mountain; and this was all the time growing wider and thicker, and rising higher, as the thunder of forty or fifty discharges per minute shook the atmosphere around Kennesaw, and reverberated from the wild Etowah hills to the crowded streets of busy, bustling, anxious Atlanta, to whose ears these sullen sounds were like the roll of the drum of fate.

Above, behind and in front of this roaring battle cloud, here and there they could see the sudden puffs of smoke which showed the explosion of the Confederate shells from the batteries on the crest of Kennesaw. These, however, were so few, comparatively, that they, as a soldier expressed it, "reminded one of a school boy throwing snowballs into a river full of ice."

But around the summit of the mountain was concentrated all the majestic terrors of the war storm.* The dense white smoke from the cannon enshrouded the parapets, the forest growth and the highest cliffs. Against the steep slopes, above the rising clouds, or in their midst, whirling them in cyclone-like circles by their explosion, the Federal shells—fuse shells, percussion shells and combination shells†—were darting like thunderbolts. At times a hundred of these seemed bursting at the same instant, and the rolling balls of smoke and the tumultuous roar were absolutely terrific. The tempest had crowned Kennesaw.

"Look!" exclaimed General Cleburne to Captains

---

*The enemy directs most of his pieces against Kennesaw. The mountain is about two miles from Marietta, and can be shelled with ease The schrapnells pass over it and far into the rear, where it has become very dangerous. Several mules and horses have been killed among the commissaries.—Augusta Constitutionalist, June 22, 1864.

† A distinguished gentleman,—a general in the Confederate army, whose command was on Kennesaw Mountain from June 20th to July 3rd, 1864, stated to the author that the Federal artillerymen used some shells,—"the like of which," said he, "I never heard of before, and have never seen since. They seemed to be what we might term combination shells; that is, they were percussion in front and fuse behind, and so arranged that if they hit anything on the mountain the cap would explode the shell; whereas, if they missed it, the shell would go flying through the air over towards Marietta, and would explode in the air when the fire from the fuse reached the powder inside.

"They were the most annoying things of the kind that I ever saw, and created not only more comment, but more damage than any other missiles the Yankees fired at us. If one hit against the mountain side, we who were up there, were in danger of their flying fragments, whereas, if they went over and exploded in the air the pieces would fall behind the mountain right into the midst of our wagon train which was immediately behind it, and as we thought when we placed it there, shelted by the mountain.

"These pieces falling would frequently hit a man or a mule, or would, anyhow, frighten the mules, and the consequence was the wagon train was in an uproar all the time. The teamsters found it much more lively than had been their expectation, or certainly their desire.

"All in all they were villainous missiles, and we had no end of annoyance from them as long as we held position on the mountain."

WAKING UP THE BATTERIES.

L. H. Mangum and Irving A. Buck, of his staff, who were intently gazing at the mountain from the centre of the works occupied by that division over a mile away; "I have seen many a thrilling spectacle during the war; but never one more sublime than this. Heaven's most appalling thunderstorm hasn't more elements of grandeur in it than yonder war cloud which has burst and is roaring around Kennesaw."

So awful was this rain of destruction that within a few minutes the Confederate batteries were practically silenced. General French ordered Major Storrs to have the guns which were not fully protected by parapets pulled back to the top of the southern slope, where the backbone of the mountain shielded them from the direct fire of the Federal artillery, and commanded the men to take shelter below them.

They were safe here from a cross-fire, since Walker's line which ran southward from the western end of Little Kennesaw was so far advanced that the Federal works in front of it were too distant for the shells from their batteries to reach the summit of the mountain. Walker's men, on the contrary, were annoyed to some extent by the shells from the Federal batteries on the north, which passed over the mountain and, exploding a thousand feet in the air, dropped their fragments in some instances into the very trenches.

For fully ten minutes after the last Confederate gun had fired the bombardment from the enemy's batteries continued with unabated fury. Trees were torn to pieces, and the falling boughs hurled clear over the mountain side; large stones were knocked from the tops of the parapets; and against monstrous crags which jutted from the summit, sometimes nearly a dozen feet high, the deadly missiles flew,—the shells exploding with sounds like thunder, and scattering fragments on every side, the solid shot chipping out huge flakes by the concussion, and then, with a ring like the curse of disappointed spite, falling impotent to the ground, or bouncing hundreds of feet down the slopes on the south.*

One poor fellow, a corporal in Ector's brigade, was killed by a cannon ball which struck a rock, glanced off over the southern side half-way down the mountain, broke off a large limb of a tree and fell upon him, mashing his skull.

* It was the second or third day before we began to realize that a Yankee could shoot to the top of Little Kennesaw: then we changed our opinions and wondered if they really meant to shoot anywhere else.—Letter from a member of Hoskins' battery to the author.

CHAPTER V.

But from the towering crest of Great Kennesaw the Confederate batteries continued belching forth defiance and destruction upon the Federals far below. Their fire was not so rapid as had been that from Little Kennesaw; on the contrary, was very deliberate, and their aim unusually precise. These had turned their attention more directly to the Federal batteries upon the two hills on opposite sides of Noonday creek, between which the Western & Atlantic Railroad runs, crossing the valley on a high, red embankment which was plainly seen from the top of the mountain.

The Federals manning the farthest of the two turned their Parrott guns against Great Kennesaw; but were fairly out-shot, and within less than twenty minutes their fire sensibly slackened, and soon theirs and the neighboring battery across the valley were silenced,—"completely knocked out," as the soldiers said.

By two or three Confederate officers who watched the scene from the summit with field-glasses the Federal gunners could be plainly observed as they pluckily worked their pieces, sending up to the mountain-top well-aimed missiles against those whose shells were exploding so accurately among and around them; but finally forsaking their death-scourged batteries and fleeing for safety into the forest behind them.

A whirlwind of enthusiastic cheers now arose from the thousands of Confederates who were surveying the scene from Great Kennesaw, and from the ravine on the west. This was renewed as their gunners next turned their attention to the Federal batteries on the hills to the east of and behind that where Tom McLellan's house now stands, less than half a mile directly in front of the eastern end of Little Kennesaw.

But as if to meet the challenge Sherman's artillerymen all along the line slackened their fire upon Little Kennesaw, and began gradually opening upon the great peak.

They first had to experiment for the range; and, their guns being elevated for the height of Little Kennesaw, the missiles struck the sides of its taller mate below the Confederate position.

There was soon an improvement, however, in this, and now from one battery and then from another, first a single shell then two or three at a time, began exploding near the crest.

Then from the Parrott battery near the Hardage house a shell, following a burst of smoke, flew, screaming like a hawk, over the very summit, and, curving downward, struck and sank into the ground in the valley on the east, and exploded just

WAKING UP THE BATTERIES.

in front of a train of cars on the Western & Atlantic Railroad, throwing mud and fragments all over the engine, and stampeding the fireman, who was "oiling up" on that side.

This engine, the "General," was the same which had been stolen at Big Shanty, April 12, 1862, by a party of twenty-two Federal soldiers in disguise, and with which they attempted the daring feat of hastening up the Western & Atlantic Railroad for the purpose of burning the bridges at its upper end.

The chase and overhauling near Ringgold, Ga., of the "General"* and her captors have become a part of the nation's history.

On the morning of this day of stirring events the "General" had taken a train load of supplies up to the Confederate lines near the foot of the mountain, and was now standing near there ready to return.

The engineer seeing the fireman "taking to the woods," sprang upon the platform, and, grasping the throttle with one hand pulled the whistle with the other, and gave a shrill blast to, as he afterward said, attract the conductor's attention.

But there was no necessity for blowing the whistle to accomplish that purpose,—the conductor already knew all about the case.

"Here, Bill," he yelled, "we'll take the fever and ague among the highlands if we stay here any longer; let's slack back to Marietta."

"Yes, I don't want my engine busted to pieces by Yankee bombshells," answered the engineer.

*The "General" is still on the Western & Atlantic Railroad, and is used for extra service.

"No," put in a countryman who was standing near, "nor I don't want my skin busted to pieces neither."

"Hold on, gentlemen," exclaimed a captain, who was having several wounded soldiers put aboard the train, "you can't go till these men are in the cars. They have got to be taken down to the hospital at Atlanta."

"Well, hurry up, Cap," said the engineer, "I'll stay here as long as you say; but I don't want to stretch it any."

"Oh, don't be afraid of a stray shell," answered the captain, "there may not be another one here in two hours."

"No, and when they do come," exclaimed one of the wounded men, "they ain't half so dangerous as a minie ball."*

Just then another shell came darting over the mountain, and exploded in the air about three hundred yards from the train.

"Make haste, Cap," yelled the engineer, "them Yankees is searching for us, and I want to find another hiding place."

* I will describe to you a new minie ball which the Yankees are using against us, and which I had exhibited to me on yesterday evening. It is made of two separate bores, one of which is a hollow shell, and the other a kind of cap from which issues a short leaden screw. On this screw is placed a loose fitting piece of tin wider than the ball itself, and very sharp. This is then fitted in the hollow shell. The object of this appears to be, that where an artery may yield to a ball it will almost to a certainty be cut by this piece of tin. But if the ball should enter a man without taking off the cap, the chances are that when it is being extracted, the tin will remain in the wound, and by constantly irritating the wound, eventually poison the flesh, and render the sufferer incurable. Such is the last devilish invention of the Yankees.—Correspondence of the Atlanta Daily Intelligencer, June 15, 1864.

WAKING UP THE BATTERIES. 81

"Oh, never mind, Bill," laughed the conductor, "they have turned in the wrong direction; let us get these poor fellows aboard, and there'll be time enough to get away."

This task was soon accomplished, however, and then at a signal from the conductor the engineer blew his whistle, and the "General" backed slowly southward toward Marietta, and in a few minutes was out of danger.

Just before she started, however, an answering whistle, as of defiance, was heard from a Federal locomotive on the same railroad, north of Kennesaw Mountain.*

General Reynolds who was near the summit of Great Kennesaw, now directed the Confederate cannoniers to turn their attention especially to the battery west of the first one which had opened, and also to see if they could not get the range of the Parrott battery near the Hardage house, which was doing the most damage of all.

Major W. C. Preston, Chief of Artillery for Walthall's division, was requested by him, during the temporary absence of the division commander from that portion of the line, to disregard the fire of the other batteries, and silence those two if possible.

Now, again the tempest of war began "blowing

---
*"The Yankees are strongly entrenched in our front, while their trains on the Western & Atlantic railroad run as near to us as two miles. During the day the shrill whistle of the engines is plainly heard over the lines, and generally elicits a hearty yell from our boys. I must confess that Sherman is a good railroad superintendent, for the prompt manner in which he has repaired the bridges over the Oostanaula and Etowah rivers prove him so."
—Correspondence of the Atlanta Daily Intelligencer, June 15, 1864.

great guns," and against Great Kennesaw the fiery messengers commenced flying from a dozen batteries.

The Confederate works, however, being slightly east of and below the immediate summit, were in a measure sheltered from the enfilading fire which the Federals attempted to bring from the guns on the extreme west of their line. Those shells either struck the western side of the crest and did no damage, or passed above the knob and flew over the heads of the Confederate gunners, and, darting into the valley, exploded, waking the echoes, but ending in noise.

It was a magnificent spectacle, however, as the shells from the mountain top, and those toward it, flew in rainbow arches, their course being frequently followed through the thick atmosphere by the smoke from their fuses, and ending in stunning explosions which filled the air with smoke and scattered the boughs from the trees, or hurled the earth and rocks in showers on every side.

With the diversion of the Federal fire from Little Kennesaw came the resolution of General French's artillerymen to reciprocate the assistance from their brothers on the other summit, and which had now brought upon Walthall's heroes the concentrated wrath of the entire Federal artillery array.

Captain Ward and Sergeant Henry Hoskins, therefore, under Major Storrs' immediate direction, had four guns run forward, and, at a given signal, fired a volley of shells at the mischievous battery

KENNESAW MOUNTAIN, FROM THE SOUTHEAST.

behind the Hardage house. The puffs of smoke above the field below showed that they had practically gotten the range of it.

"Now, gentlemen," said General French, who had noticed that the Federal batteries were all turned against Great Kennesaw, "hurry up, and pour in a few dozen shells before they can face our way again."

The men uttering a thrilling yell, pushed all the guns forward, tramping through the beds of prickly pear with their almost bare feet, regardless of the cruel thorns, and with wonderful alacrity opened upon the Federal position below.

For three or four minutes not a missile came in response; but then the hissing scream of a shell was heard above them, and the next instant the deafening explosion followed, and one of the soldiers on the farther slope of the ridge fell, with his leg badly bruised.

"Keep it up, boys," shouted Major Storrs, "draw some of that fire which they've got against Great Kennesaw. The boys helped us, so we must help them out!"

"Yes, we'll do it," yelled the men, "they've got to divide with us. Clear out of the way of the Yallerhammers, Yanks."

"Yallerhammers" was the nickname given Captain Ward's brass Napoleon guns by the soldiers in this division.

And now again the uproar from the guns on the crest of Little Kennesaw was renewed, and with

WAKING UP THE BATTERIES. 85

marked effect, for within a few minutes one of the Federal batteries was silenced by their fire.

Captain Hoskins' gunners on the right of the line turned their attention to a column of Federal infantry and a wagon train with a large drove of cattle which was passing down the road behind their batteries. Sergeant George Duke, with Preston Keys, Ben King, Zach Hoskins, J. F. Smith, and Wess Graham in charge of "Gun No. 1," and Sergeant Henry Hoskins, with Gus Furr, Has Furr, Bob Cornega and the "three Jims" (Rutland, Allen and Smith), with "Gun No. 2," under Major Storrs' personal supervision, did themselves proud.

Elevating the guns to an angle of forty-five degrees, they sent their shells beyond the position occupied by the artillery, and began dropping them into the midst of the moving column.

Great excitement was instantly apparent among the cattle and in the wagon train; and one or two officers, with field-glasses, saw the teams going at nearly every angle across the open field by the road.

The infantry also began double-quicking, and breaking up into detachments which got out of range as rapidly as possible, while the cattle, left to themselves, were stampeded by the bursting bombs, and scattered in a hundred directions.

While this was going on Guibor's battery was being worked as usual for all it was worth. Several notably fine shots were made by Sergeants Lawrence, Murphy and Robinson and by Pat Quinn. One of the shells sent by Pat exploded right under one of the enemy's guns, and when the smoke cleared away, the gun was seen lying on its side out of its previous location.

But the triumph of the Confederates was only temporary, for the explosion of shells and the crashing of solid shot among the crags about their ears, soon told them that the boys on Great Kennesaw had been forced "to divide with them." In fact, the Federals leaving only about three batteries to play upon Great Kennesaw, had turned again almost their entire fury against the western summit.

So terrific did this become that a second time the Confederates withdrew their guns to the south side of the crest.

"It's hard for nine guns to whip a hundred and twenty-five or fifty!" exclaimed Major Storrs, as the men once more retired for shelter behind the jutting crags. It was well that they "lay low" and hugged the southern cliffs, for the bombardment had become absolutely fearful. The mountain was crowned with the fiery tempest, and tumult and destruction reigned supreme.

In the midst of this scene of terror occurred an incident so startling, so thrilling, that it almost curdled the blood of every one who beheld it.

Little Jack Harper, the eight-year-old "pet of the camp," who had been sheltered with his sister behind a crag, through a crevice in the rock saw the flagstaff on the parapet struck by a shell and shattered to splinters. The starry cross of silk, with the upper fragment of the staff, was whirled

WAKING UP THE BATTERIES. 87

nearly twenty feet backward, and fell to the ground.

Like a flash Jack darted from his cover, and, grasping the banner, exclaimed, as indignant tears burst from his eyes, "Oh, you bad old Yankees, you've knocked down our flag; but I'll put it back again!"

With this childish shout he rushed forward amid the thunder and smoke of the explosion of a score of shells, and, climbing up the rocky sides of the parapet, stood upon its very top, and then, facing the "bad old Yankees" on the north, with both hands waved the banner of Dixie back and forward in delirious triumph.

A freezing shriek of horror rang out amid the tumult; and the score of soldiers and officers who had just sprung forward to jerk the child from his perch, stood transfixed with dismay, as Jack's sister, Miss Mary Harper, who had also been sheltered behind the same crag with the boy, rushed forward into the midst of the smoke and danger toward him.

At that instant, however, a shell from a Federal battery exploded in the midst of the boughs of a tree in front of her, with a terrific report, amid a cloud of smoke which completely hid Jack, and scattered the debris in every direction. A whole section of the tree was hurled to the ground, falling against the parapet behind the boy, and between him and his now half-crazed sister, and obstructing her course toward him.

With her hands clasped convulsively above her head, she screamed, "Merciful God, protect my darling baby brother!"

But now like a whirlwind there was a general rush toward the two. John Minon seized the frantic girl in his arms, and bore her, fainting, back behind the bowlders. Captain Ward leaned upon the parapet and caught Jack, who was jumping around, and yelling in boyish glee, as he swung the colors backward and forward: "Oh, yes, you bad old Yankees, you thought our flag was down; but HERE IT IS, waving right before you. Yes, HERE IT IS; don't you see it?"

As he was dragged backward, he "struggled like a young wild cat," as one of the soldiers expressed it, and cried in thrilling tones of grief, "Oh! don't, oh! let me alone; they'll think we've surrendered, and we haven't! don't you see our flag's down on the ground now? Let me 'loose, so I can put it up again!"

"Never mind, Jack," shouted Captain Ward, "I'll put the flag up. We haven't surrendered."

"And we don't intend to, do we, Captain?" exclaimed Jack, with his eyes flashing like diamonds, as he threw his arms around the neck of the brave commander, on discovering who he was; "but where are you going to put the flag?"

"I'll put it just where you had it, Jack," answered Captain Ward, as he set the boy in his former retreat. "Now do you stay here, and the flag will soon be waving all right."

WAKING UP THE BATTERIES. 89

"Hurrah for the South and our flag!" shouted Jack, as the captain with the colors now hastily left him.

"Yes, hurrah for the South and for our flag, Jack!" exclaimed Captain Ward, "and, Jack, stay just where you are. Those are my orders."

"All right, I'll obey," answered the boy, "I'll obey."

"My God! Minon," exclaimed Captain Ward, as he turned and saw the latter with one hand, bearing Miss Mary Harper's unconscious form toward shelter, "what is this? is she hurt?"

"No, sir, I think she's only fainted; but a piece of shell has just broken my right arm," said the young soldier, glancing at that member which was hanging loosely by his side.

"God grant she be not hurt! but let me help you," answered the captain, as he clasped the young lady tenderly in his arms, and hurried back with her, "come on, Minon."

They darted behind the huge rock, just as a solid shot went crashing through a tree, hurling a large branch forward, whose foliage knocked the captain's hat off, and scratched his neck as it passed.

Paying no attention to this, however, he laid the young lady upon a blanket before Jack, who burst into a flood of tears, and screamed, "Oh, have those bad old Yankees killed my sister? oh, Captain, have they killed her?"

"No, Jack," answered the captain, "I hope she is not hurt. I think she has only fainted. Minon, please hand me your canteen, if you have any water in it."

"I haven't any, Captain, but I will run and get some," said the latter.

"No, let me go," shouted Jack, "I'll bring some from the bucket near the cannon."

"Hold!" exclaimed Captain Ward, grasping the boy by the shoulder, "I ordered you to stay behind here; and you promised to obey,—I don't allow any of my soldiers to disobey my orders."

"All right, Captain, I beg your pardon, and will obey," answered Jack, "but I wanted so much to help sister."

"That wish does you honor, my dear boy," said the commander, patting him on the head; "but here we have the water now, Mr. Minon has brought it. Now bring her once more to consciousness while I redeem my promise, and put back the flag where you had it. Matthews is down to the left helping to work gun number four," he added, speaking to himself.

"I'm ahead of ye, Captain, this time!" shouted Partridge, who had seized the colors while the gallant artillery leader was doing the doubly gallant act toward Miss Harper, "I helped to fetch on this row, and now I'm going to help see it through creditably."

With this remark he plunged forward through the smoke, and, waved the banner to and fro, and then, leaning forward, placed it against the stump of a sapling, and, leisurely pulling a strong cord

WAKING UP THE BATTERIES. 91

from his pocket, tied the remnant of the staff to the top. Then swinging his hat aloft, he looked toward the enemy's batteries, and yelled defiantly, "Thar, dern ye, knock it down ag'in if ye can!"

This done, he leaped to the ground, behind the

PARTRIDGE.

works, and exclaiming, "It tires me down to play the hero long at a time!" darted like a stag to the shelter of the rocks on the south.

"Now let everybody keep behind shelter and behave himself," exclaimed Major Storrs, who had beheld the latter part of this episode, "Let there be no more exposure to danger till I give the order."

He had scarcely made this remark before he turned around and noticed, coming up the southern slope, General Loring and one of his orderlies. The major at once stepped downward and met him with the remark:

"If you have been getting cold come up here and we will let you see what it is to have a warm time."

"Thank you, Major," said General Loring, "I think this is hot enough for all the requirements of a reasonable man. But what seems to be the idea of the Yankees in this tremendous uproar from their batteries?"

"Oh, well," said the major, "you can't always judge what a lot of fellows are intending when they are kicking up a fuss nearly a mile away from you."

"But how many guns have they playing upon you to-day?" asked General Loring.

"Oh, I think they have the full quota of one hundred and twenty-five or fifty," answered the major. "But if you would like to see for yourself how it looks in the forests and on the hill-tops below us, I will walk down with you to our big rock, and we will mount that and see with our own eyes."

"All right," said the general, "let us venture over there for a few minutes."

So saying the two officers and the orderly walked westward to Observation Rock. Major Storrs climbed upon it, and then reached his hand down and said, "General, let me give you a lift."

"Thank you," said General Loring, "I can't climb so well with one arm as you can with two.

WAKING UP THE BATTERIES. 93

Ah! by the way, isn't this the very rock upon which you stood and counted the Yankee guns two or three days ago?"*

"Yes, sir," answered the major, "that was the time when poor McBride was killed."

The three stood upon the rock, and Major Storrs first took his field-glass and gave it a sweep around the smoke-obscured country down in front. Handing it then to the general, he remarked:

"You needn't take the trouble to count them, for I am sure all the dogs of war are barking at us. But look yonder to the north, General. See that train on the railroad, which has just come down from Big Shanty. I can plainly see it with the naked eye, and can hear its rumbling between cannon shots. See that little jet of smoke, and hear that whistle blowing 'down brakes.' They had better put on the brakes before they get under fire from our batteries. The train is scarcely two miles from us, and some of the big guns on the other peak might possibly reach it."

"Yes," replied General Loring, "it has come to a dead stop; and, see the soldiers pouring out of it! A sort of blue fringe is all around it. Now they are forming into line. I suppose they are going

---

*"After we had been on the mountain several days, and the enemy continuing to accumulate artillery in our front, Gen. Johnston directed Gen. French to have their guns counted.

"Gen. French directed me to go upon the mountain, open fire so as to develop the enemy's full force of artillery, and count his guns. This I did, taking position on an elevated point, a large rock, I believe, to the left of my batteries, so as to be out of the smoke of my guns, and with a pair of field-glasses, I counted the enemy's pieces over several times until I was perfectly satisfied that one hundred and forty were playing upon us at that time."— Major Geo. S. Storrs in letter to the author.

down to take position in front of Featherston. Well, let them come, we are ready for them."

"Yes," answered Major Storrs, "let them come along as soon as they will."

The general silently scanned the scene below with the glass for about five or six minutes. During this time the shells were screaming and bursting over and on all sides of them. Some of the soldiers had raised their heads above the rocks, and looked with considerable interest at the daring of the three, and Lieutenant Billy Richardson of Ward's battery, remarked to those beside him:

"Whenever you're hunting for brave men and come to Major Storrs and General Loring, you can stop, for there's no need of going any further."

After standing upon the rock some three or four minutes, General Loring laughed, and said to Major Storrs:

"Well, I expect, for a corps commander, I have stood up here as a mark for their shells long enough, and that there is no strict necessity for General Polk's successor to court his fate."

"Yes," said Major Storrs, "and I don't see any real necessity for a division chief of artillery to remain here, just at this particular juncture, any longer than is proper to demonstrate to his higher officer that his batteries are under a pretty heavy fire from guns superior in number and calibre."

"Oh! I always know where this chief of artillery is to be found whenever there is any tough fighting going on; but I don't think a man is always safe

WAKING UP THE BATTERIES. 95

who stays by his side too long after he has found him," answered the General.

With a mutual smile the three then climbed down to the ground, and hastily made their way over to the southern side of the mountain.

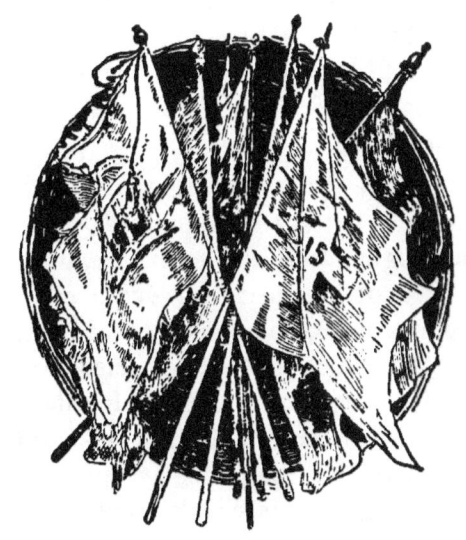

CHAPTER VI.

Major Storrs, Generals Loring and French then walked behind the crest of the ridge to the slope leading into the ravine on the southeast. They here met General Ector, who, with a couple of members of his staff, was coming to consult General French; and all six now, going forward amid the forest growth, could observe the general direction of the Federal fire.

This was once more seeking the crest of Great Kennesaw, and battery after battery was turning a portion of its guns from the lower summit toward it.

Major Preston's object, however, had already been, in a measure accomplished, as the steady and deliberate fire which he had directed against the battery of Parrott guns near the Hardage house, had proven so disastrous that it had apparently driven the men from the guns, except one piece to the left, which still at intervals, replied, and with some effect.

But as the four officers, and a few others who accompanied them, surveyed the great crest, the dense white clouds which were rising from it for hundreds of yards into the air, and the sudden puffs of smoke from shells which flew screaming over their heads and burst thick and fast amid the forest on its slope, accompanied by the sharp report of the explosion, and the ringing, crashing sound of the scattering fragments against the rocks or through the trees, told them that the war-tempest was once more drifting against the great mountain.

The fury of this storm suddenly rose in its intensity to the raging and appalling roar of the whirlwind, as the hitherto silent casemated battery on the east side of the railroad and another, not previously known to have been built, became enveloped in white smoke from the simultaneous discharge of all of their pieces, and their deadly shells, aimed with remarkable precision, exploded almost in the very midst of the upper tier of Preston's guns. Again and yet again those fiery monsters, securely sheltered under the ground, belched forth death and ruin around the mountain top. Hidden themselves and safe from harm, they seemed to find every weak point in the Confederate works, and the very lightning appeared as flashing forth from the rocks on the parapets as their terrific shells came dashing against them and shattering them to atoms.

It was certainly a grand scene, and from their shelter above the ravine the officers could without danger to themselves take in all its terrific majesty.

They remained for some ten minutes beholding the rapid increase of the shower of shells and other missiles, which now fringed the entire peak with patches of cloud and flying boughs which were torn from the trees, when suddenly from near the summit a dense column of smoke and fire shot up hundreds of feet above it, and then ensued a stunning report which nearly deafened every one who heard.

The fire of the Confederate batteries almost instantly ceased, and with the naked eye they could observe great commotion among the men on the side of the mountain; as a whole brigade, apparently, rushed forward to the scene of disaster and ruin, while the shouts from their midst told that the event was one of unusual moment.

"Hurry over at once, and see what has happened," said General French to an orderly, "I think a shell has dropped into Major Preston's ammunition and exploded it. Go down behind the ridge to your right, so as to be sheltered from the Yankee fire; and return as soon as possible."

Tipping his hat, the young subaltern hurried away, and was soon lost to view amid the undergrowth. They saw him again in a few minutes, climbing the heights on the southern side of the great peak, and shortly thereafter he disappeared behind the knob.

About this time General Loring remarked to General French, "I don't think I'll wait for a report to be sent here as to the occurrence over yonder, but will go myself. I presume that it is only an ammunition chest or something of that kind which has been exploded by a Yankee shell."

WAKING UP THE BATTERIES.

"I have no doubt," said General French, "that you are correct."

"Yes, beyond all question," said Major Storrs, "and I can hardly believe that anything serious is the matter on the other peak."

"Well, it will take but a few minutes to find out," said General Loring, "so, good morning, gentlemen, I will see you at a later time."

So saying, he walked down the southern side of the ridge at a rapid pace.

Just at this period, however, occurred an incident which was so thoroughly ludicrous in some of its features that the three officers in the midst of their anxiety, because of the catastrophe on the other peak, could not restrain their risibilities. Two soldiers, who had been sent into the valley on the south for water for their comrades, had just reached the top of the slope on their way back. About a hundred canteens were swung to a pole which they were carrying on their shoulders. A shell passed between the two, struck the pole and whirled it from them back down toward Marietta, and, exploding, scattered the canteens, as one of them said, "all over north Georgia." The clatter of the tin, the swish of the spilling water, as they were blown to pieces, and the crash of the bursting shell were remembered for many a day. Strange to say neither of the water carriers was hurt.

In the meantime, after only four or five minutes' cessation, the batteries on Great Kennesaw opened again, first with one gun, then with four others.

The Federal bombardment, however, had known no rest; on the contrary, during the silent interval among the Confederates, the enemy's shells had poured with unceasing fury around them.

But the knob of the peak, as before shown, had prevented this from proving as dreadful a scourge as had been the case on Little Kennesaw, inasmuch as the Federal batteries in general were located more to the west of it, and their shells, therefore, either struck that face of the peak, doing no damage, or generally passed far beyond it before exploding.

Major Preston, taking advantage of the location, had brought forward two guns, and, placing them on the gradual incline below the crest, to the left of where the casemated battery's shells were constantly exploding, had, by elevating them, opened fire over the summit upon the Federal position westward.

They discharged several shells, while a couple of the men with field-glasses on the northern side of the mountain watched and reported where they fell. At length they secured the range of a battery which faced Little Kennesaw, and Major Preston then ordered these two pieces to keep up their play upon that location.

Thus the tumultuous combat was continuing when the orderly returned, and reported that Major Preston had stated to him that the cause of the catastrophe, about which General French had made inquiry, was the falling of a Federal shell into the midst of an ammunition chest which was behind the guns on the crest of the mountain. This and another were side by side, each having thirty-two rounds of ammunition. They had both exploded with a terrific concussion,* blowing trees to pieces, hurling huge bowlders like pebbles over the cliffs, knocking men flat to the ground for fifty yards around, and, like a volcano, shooting a column of fire, smoke and debris hundreds of feet into the air.

By one of those strange mercies of Providence, however, but few men were in the immediate vicinity of the chests; consequently only two were known to be killed and four wounded. One of the former was blown over the southern side of the mountain and his body, with head and one arm off, was found lodged amid the branches of a tree nearly a hundred yards below.

Just after this report was received, General French observed an officer coming up the ravine from the south, whom he recognized as Colonel R. J. Manning, a member of General Johnston's staff.

"Good morning, Colonel," he exclaimed, saluting him at the same time, "come this way, please. Are you from headquarters?"

"Yes, General," answered Colonel Manning, "General Johnston has sent me to ascertain the cause of this extraordinary bombardment, and to

---

*This explosion, a Confederate officer, who was present and an eye-witness, states to the author to have been one of the grandest and most fearful sights of its kind which he beheld during four years of war.

know if you need any assistance from other parts of the line. Are the Yankees covering any movement of infantry by this artillery fire?"

"No, sir," replied General French, "I think they are merely in for an artillery duel to-day, and are attempting to silence our batteries on the mountain top. You can say to General Johnston that we have infantry force strong enough to more than check any assault which they might dare; but there is, I think, no danger of an assault."

"Well, at any rate," observed Colonel Manning, "they are playing their guns for all they are worth. I have had a very dangerous journey coming from headquarters up here. The shells are flying over the mountain, exploding sometimes a thousand feet in the air and scattering their fragments all around, or are lighting in the forest below and tearing whole trees to pieces. It is more dangerous down yonder for half a mile than it is on the slope near the summit. I'll go with you awhile and see how it looks up here, so that I can report to General Johnston as an eye-witness as well as the bearer of your message. This is a spectacle worth climbing a mountain to behold."

"Yes," said Major Storrs, "the bombardment of a mountain top is a rare scene in military affairs."

"But what is the status of affairs at other parts of the line, Colonel?" asked General French.

"Nothing serious," answered the latter. "The Yankees are throwing a good many shells over our line from their position east of the railroad,* and they have just tried our position on Hardee's front without success."

"Yes," said General French, "I saw that attack from up here."

General French and his party now walked back to their post on Little Kennesaw, and Major Storrs was directed to run one or two guns forward at a time at different places on the ridge, and open upon the Federals, the object being to prevent the concentration of their fire upon the Confederate position on Great Kennesaw.

They soon met Captain Ward and Lieutenant Harris, and Major Storrs gave them the programme, and sent similar orders to Hoskins' section of two guns on the mountain top and to his and Bellamy's batteries, on the hill west of Little Kennesaw, commanding the Burnt Hickory road.

As they separated, the major noticed Captain Ward shake his head in a jocular manner, and say to the sharpshooter, Partridge, who was standing by his side, "You had better get down in front of the mountain; we are going to 'wake up the batteries,' and those Yankees want to shoot especially

*The Yankees, by marching and counter-marching, have succeeded in maneuvering into possession of a portion of the ridge which stretches off to the right from the railroad, and overlooking Marietta. By these open movements by day and counter moves by night they have advanced their lines considerably, though not, perhaps, very advantageously, on our wings; but on our centre they have gained only a few hundred yards of advance. Whether it will be an advantage time will develop. The enemy has learned to his great cost that our retention of the mountain is most destructive and formidable to him. He is chary of attack on the centre. Our terrible batteries and formidable engines of destruction are against their advance, and hitherto the impregnable point has only been bombarded.—Atlanta Intelligencer, June 22, 1864.

at you. They'd rather hit you than to dismount all the cannon on Kennesaw."

"Yes, Gosh dern 'em!" was the response, "you make out like you're a jokin'; but onbeknownst you're tellin' the solidest kind of facts and truth. I tell ye what, when they first begun drappin' the'r shells around, amongst the rocks, I laughed; yes, I fairly haw-hawed. But after 'while I jest sorter smiled, and then, when they commenced a rainin' down bustin' bombshells, like fire and brimstone on Sodom and Gomorry; and when the very rocks seemed to be spittin' out flames, and when the smoke from the whole mountain and the surroundin' kentry went up like the smoke of a furnace, I knowed the best place for me was on this side of Kennesaw. I don't know how I got through the gap, but I'm here to show I did."

"Yes, but you are not as badly frightened as you pretend," laughed the captain; and added, "true merit is always modest."

"Oh, I ain't skeered now; but I acknowledge the corn I was then," replied Partridge, with a grin. "But, hello, boys, what the mischief's the matter?" he exclaimed, running forward amid a group of soldiers who had jumped up in a confused manner from behind a huge rock, one of them pointing his musket toward the ground and firing it.

"Rattlesnake!" answered several in a breath.

"But I done for him, consarn his rusty side," said the one who had fired, pointing at the writhing reptile whose head was nearly cut off by the well-directed bullet.

"He came from under the rock right among us," said a lieutenant to Major Storrs, who had stepped forward to see what was the cause of the excitement.

"We're in a nice trap," interjected a soldier, "Yankees shooting at us in front, rattlesnakes biting at us from behind, and cactus sticking our feet from underneath."

"Yes, and the devil playing his pranks on every side," said the lieutenant.

"And still we'll whip the fight," exclaimed Major Storrs in a cheery tone.

" "Yes, that is, we'll undertake to whip the rattlesnakes and the Yankees, and mash down the cactus, if the Lord will manage the devil," added Captain Ward, with a laugh.

The party then dispersed and went to their several posts.

Within a few minutes one of Captain Hoskins' pieces was discharged, and a shell was landed near the Federal works below.

One of Ward's guns, aimed by Lieutenant William ("Billy") Richardson, who was one of the crack marksmen of the artillery battalion, was next fired, and its shell was seen, through the glasses, to knock a small log cabin, just behind one of the batteries, to pieces, causing a stampede by several men who were in it.

Guibor's battery followed suit, and the enemy

was put on notice that the mountain was still held by "the unterrified."

An irregular fire was now kept up from Little Kennesaw by the Confederates, "stealing a shot now and then," as Major Storrs termed it, which drew away the attention of the Federal batteries to some extent from Great Kennesaw, and thus accomplished the result sought by General French. One of Hoskins' guns, aimed by Major Storrs himself, blew up a caisson right in the very midst of the battery east of Tom McLellan's house.

But, after another furious bombardment of the western crest from nearly all their guns, which was comparatively barren of results, except in making a magnificent display, the Federal fire gradually slackened until at about sunset it ceased entirely.

The Confederates had drawn back their guns and did not fire a single round from Little Kennesaw during the last half hour, and from the higher peak only an occasional shell was thrown in return. They had too scant a supply of ammunition to use it in mere artillery duels.

Both officers and men watched the gradual cessation of the fiery tempest, and noticed how battery after battery became silent on the hills below; and then, with the danger over, crowded on top of the ridge again, standing in the open spaces, or mounting the huge bowlders, to survey the inspiring scenes around and beneath them.

The sun was just disappearing beneath the horizon. Yet not in the quiet majesty of a clear day was his golden disc kissing the hill-tops, but, as typical of the tumultuous events of the hours he had illumined, the dazzling orb was sinking into the embrace of a stormy sea of clouds whose conquering waves, dashed high into the air, his glittering rays were gilding with roses and fire.

From Lost Mountain on the right a column of fleecy mists seemed towering far, far upward toward the zenith; and from out its ruddy sides a thousand silvery banners hung their wavy pennons of light which radiated from pearls, opals, diamonds, rubies and topazes garnishing their borders. Circling in a majestic arch from north to south fold after fold of golden fleece bounded the cerulean expanse; while scattered in indescribable disarray appeared castles, mountains, placid lakes, rainbows and surging billows of roseate hue. A myriad clusters of light were playing around their sides and crowning their crests.

Back of all these, in the sky above, thick inky-hued masses of clouds were drifting together, as if threatening another storm such as had pelted the mountain and its occupants so dismally the night before.

But no rain was destined to come "between suns' now, although obscurity was drawing his misty robes around Kennesaw and its rival armies, and the clammy kiss of sable night was almost imprinted upon the eastern forests below them.

CHAPTER VII.

And now while, so far as regarded the tremendous engines of war:

"Silence settled deep and still
O'er the lone wood and mighty hill,"

the tender emotions of chivalrous manhood found their homes in the hearts of Captain Ward and those immediately around him.

Leaving his guns, he had gone behind the sheltering bowlder, where Miss Mary Harper had been left with little Jack and John Minon to restore her to consciousness from the fainting fit into which she had gone in the midst of the terrifically thrilling episode, in which Jack had figured as the hero.

The sun had scarcely disappeared when he stepped quietly around with the question, "Well, how are the queen of Kennesaw and the champion of the flag of Dixie?"

"Oh! Captain Ward," shouted Jack jumping up, and running to his side, "we've whipped the Yankees, haven't we? We've still got the mountain and our cannon; and our flag is still waving, isn't it? Haven't we whipped 'em, Captain?"

"Yes, Jack," laughed the captain, taking the

WAKING UP THE BATTERIES. 109

enthusiastic youngster up into his arms, "we've kept off the Yankees, and we've got all of our cannon and the mountain; and our flag is still waving just where you had it. Ah! Miss Harper," he added, turning to her and watching her as she was wrapping a new bandage around the arm of Minon, "was the poet referring to you when he wrote:

'A ministering angel thou!'"

"No, indeed! Captain," she quickly replied with a merry laugh; "that was written some fifty or sixty years ago; and surely you don't mean to insinuate that you think I look that old."

"Perish the thought! never, never, no, never would I be guilty of an insinuation so utterly devoid of foundation as that" he exclaimed, and then added:

"But you know the language of prophecy sometimes reads like it refers to the day in which it is given forth; and thus Sir Walter builded wiser than he knew when he wrote the words which fit her to whom I now speak. Minon, you are a lucky chap. But for the anxiety it would give my dear wife and little ones at home, I almost wish I had been wounded, so that I too could have had the attention of so fair a nurse,—one who seems to have been wafted from the clouds into our midst to cheer and to save."

"You say you almost wish; now, Captain, I go farther than that, and say that I am not sorry I was wounded; because the privilege of having such a nurse counterbalances the pain of the wound."

"But, it does not counterbalance to our country the loss of the power of your arm in this day of her trial and need," said Miss Harper in a tone almost of reproach, "therefore you should be very sorry that you are disabled, while your brothers around you are still strong and ready to battle for her cause."

"Nobly spoken, Miss Harper!" exclaimed Captain Ward, clapping his hands, "I am glad to see somebody besides myself turned down in your neat manner; and then that is the correct doctrine for this time and occasion."

"I surrender!" ejaculated Minon, "I am not only defeated, but discomfited. There's no answer to that except one."

"And," said Miss Harper, "that is"—

"To get well at the very earliest possible minute, and scamper back to my place at the front."

"Well, no one will be more delighted to see you get well than I," was the gentle answer; "and I am willing to depend upon you to carry out the latter part of your promise, when your strength and health are restored."

"Te-ump, te-ump, te-ump, te-tump!" hummed Captain Ward, in a tone of assumed indifference, and with a comical twinkle in his eye; and added,

"Jack, it's getting rather close behind this rock; hadn't we two better walk forward into the open air? There's more room for us out there, I think."

WAKING UP THE BATTERIES. 111

"No, no indeed, Captain"! exclaimed the young lady with a blush, "those were only such words as every woman should speak to every Southern gentleman."

"Yes, Captain Ward," said Jack springing to his feet, "Let's go forward among the cannon, and see what the old Yankees are doing. Our men whipped 'em, didn't we?"

"Oh! we whipped them badly, Jack," replied the captain.

"Hold on, Jack!" exclaimed his sister with a start, "you shan't go forward into the jaws of danger again. Come, we must return to Marietta before any more trouble comes upon us. Mother will be almost crazy about us, and we must go at once."

"Oh! no, Sis," answered Jack impetuously, as tears gushed from his eyes, "there's no danger now, and I do want to go and see over the mountain at the Yankees. Captain Ward told me to come on; and he'll take good care of me."

"Yes, let us go for a minute, Miss Harper," said the captain, "there is no danger just now. Come with us, too, and survey the pomp of war, since you have already seen and heard its terrors."

"Well, I will go for a few minutes, and then Jack and I must be getting away from here. This is no place for women and children."

They started forward toward the parapet.

"Stop a minute," said Miss Mary, "do listen to that red-bird. I thought every one of his kind had flown at least five miles away from the mountain after the terrible tumult which had surrounded it to-day. But the little fellow has lit upon that tree, and is singing as fearlessly and merrily as though a cannon had never been fired in Georgia."

"Yes," said Captain Ward, "he is a regular Confederate. It takes something more than a bombardment from Yankee batteries to demoralize him."

"Ah!" interjected a soldier standing right by them, "that's the right kind of talk; but I confess that for awhile I felt like the fellow did up about Chickamauga. He saw a dog skedaddling through the woods as fast as his legs could carry him when the battle was about at its worst. Stopping for an instant, he looked at him, and then said in an under tone, 'Run, dog, run, if I wasn't a man I'd run too.'"

A hearty laugh ensued from the party, after which Miss Harper remarked, "But our little redbird is made of more heroic stuff than the dog in your story."

The bright little winged songster, as if almost conscious of the fact that he was receiving such flattering attention, continued warbling forth some of his gayest and sweetest notes. Then, stopping for an instant, he arose from his perch, darted over toward the right, and, alighting upon the very muzzle of one of the cannon of Guibor's battery, which was now temporarily deserted, resumed his inspiring little song. A hundred eyes beheld him, and there

WAKING UP THE BATTERIES. 113

was apparently a general desire to applaud the little Confederate prototype; but all refrained until after a couple of minutes' flow of his merriest notes, he arose and flew still further toward the right of the line. Then there was a general clapping of hands and an enthusiastic cheer with shouts of "Hurrah for our game little Confederate!" and Partridge shook his head and emphatically exclaimed, "I'll never shoot another red-bird!"

As they walked up toward the northern side of the ridge, the sound of a banjo and the patter of feet were heard near by, and, passing a huge bowlder, they suddenly came upon a group of soldiers around a negro who was picking a banjo and singing, while a couple of other negroes were patting and dancing a jig.

The soldiers, seeing the lady, immediately arose, throwing off their air of abandon and carelessness, and saluted her and her escort with respectful deference. The darkeys, however, being so busily engaged in amusing the party, did not notice what was the cause of the uprising, and continued their merriment.

As Captain Ward and the others passed along, they caught one verse of the negro's song:

> "Rabbit take his pipe to smoke,
> 'Coon eat turkey hash;
> 'Possum try to crack a joke,
> But wolf run off wid de cash."

Jack was immensely amused at this part of the

proceedings, and lingered to hear some more of it; but the others passed on their way.

Within a minute or so, however, he came running forward and exclaimed in a pleading tone: "O, Captain Ward, and Sis, please come back here and listen to the singing; it's mighty funny."

Well, Jack," answered the captain good-humoredly, "I reckon we will have to hear a song or two for your especial benefit,—a sort of mountain concert in the open air by uneducated artistes."

They accordingly stepped back among the merry makers who again rose to greet them.

Captain Ward then remarked, "Don't let us break up the fun, boys; we have come to enjoy it with you. And you have the most select audience you ever rehearsed before. Now, Woodson, give us one of your best, and do your best."

"All right, Marse John, we'll do our level best; but what song does you want? How'll 'Susanna do for yer?" said Woodson.

"That'll do finely," exclaimed the captain, "Now do you play and sing, and we'll all join in the chorus."

"Yes, sir," said Jack, "we'll all join in the chorus."

"All right, Jack," added Miss Harper with a laugh, "we'll all join in the chorus for your benefit."

The whole party formed a circle around Woodson, who began picking his banjo, and then sang:

"Ise come from Alabama wid de banjo on my knee,
Ise gwine to Louisiana my true love for to see;

WAKING UP THE BATTERIES.   115

It rain'd all night de day I left, de wedder it was dry,
De sun so hot I froze to deaf, Susanna, don't you cry."

Then as Woodson threw back his head, walled his eyes, patted his feet and slung his banjo around in a serio-comic ecstacy, the entire line of officers, privates, negroes and Jack and his sister stormed out the chorus:

"O Susanna!
  Don't you cry for me;
  I've come from Alabama
  With the banjo on my knee."

After picking his banjo nimbly for a minute, Woodson wagged his head in what may best be termed a zig-zag manner, and sang the second verse:

"I jump'd aboard de Telegraph an' travel'd down de river,
 De 'lectric fluid magnified and killed four hundred nigger,
 De bullgine bust, de hoss run off, I really thought to die;
 I shot my eyes to hold my breff; Susanna, don't you cry."

Officers and men now joined "all hands 'round," and with the patter of feet woke the welkin with:

"O Susanna!
  Don't you cry for me;
  I've come from Alabama
  With the banjo on my knee."

Jack laughed till he almost choked; and Woodson, after a broad grin had shown his big white teeth, continued in a rather subdued tone:

"I had a dream de odder night when everything was still,
 I thought I seen Susanna a comin' down de hill,
 De buckwheat cake war in her mouf, de tear war in her eye,
 Says I, 'Ise comin' from de Souf, Susanna, don't you cry."

Just here every man put his hand to his mouth,

after Captain Ward had whispered to Miss Harper, and Jack found himself the only one singing the chorus.

> "O Susanna!
> Don't you cry for me—"

his childish voice rang out, shrill and clear; but, hearing no others, and seeing a solemn look upon the faces of all, and every one perfectly silent, Jack exclaimed:

"Oh! ain't you going to sing the chorus? Excuse me."

All were provokingly quiet for about twenty seconds, while Jack's face became as red as a beet; but then Captain Ward came to his relief by shouting:

> "O Susanna!"

and the entire circle joined in, and shook the air with,

> "Don't you cry for me;
> I've come from Alabama
> With the banjo on my knee."

Woodson after an instant picked his banjo, and continued:

"I'll soon be down in New Orleens, an' den I'll look all 'round,
  An' if I find Susanna I'll fall upon de ground;
  But if I do not find her dis darkey'll shorely die,
  And when I'm dead and buried, Susanna, don't you cry."

Woodson then jumped up, swung his banjo above his head, and, as the other negroes patted vigorously, began dancing an old-fashioned jig, while all of his audience swung their hats above their heads and, marching around in a circle, sang:

>"O Susanna!
>Don't you cry for me;
>I've come from Alabama
>With the banjo on my knee."

The echoes seemed to linger among the crags, and Jack laughed himself almost hoarse. He then turned to Captain Ward and said:

"O Captain, now get Sis to sing, 'O yes, I am a Southern girl.' I know these soldiers would like to hear it."

"Oh! no, indeed, Jack," exclaimed his sister, "you will be voted a first-class nuisance if you don't hold your tongue."

"Ah! but why not, Miss Harper? I like Jack's suggestion, and dare say that all these gentlemen would feel honored and delighted if you would sing for us. Pardon me for saying that you have illustrated the highest type of Southern womanhood to-day, and I am sure we would all be charmed to have you sing for us."

"Yes, please sing for us; we should so much like to hear you," came from at least twenty voices in the throng.

"Well, this is more than I bargained for," said the young lady to Captain Ward, while her face was suffused with blushes, "But I am without an accompaniment."

"Ah, we will supply that," answered the captain. "Here, Mr. Carnes, please bring your cornet."

"With great pleasure, sir," exclaimed the young musician, who was a member of the division band, and a superb master of his art.

Stepping forward, he bowed politely to Miss Harper, who smiled and said, "If 'twere done 'twere well 'twere done quickly."

Taking his cornet, he began playing the prelude to the air, "The bonnie blue flag," and then, as its clear, silvery echoes quivered around the mountain top with the sweetest melody, Miss Harper sang:

> "Oh! yes, I am a Southern girl,
>   And glory in the name,
> And boast it with far greater pride
>   Than glittering wealth or fame.
> We envy not the Northern girl,
>   Her robes of beauties rare,
> Though diamonds grace her snowy neck,
>   And pearls bedeck her hair.
>
> Chorus.—Hurrah! hurrah!
>   For the sunny South so dear:
>   Three cheers for the homespun dress
>   The Southern ladies wear.
>
> The homespun dress is plain, I know,
>   My hat's palmetto, too;
> But then it shows what Southern girls
>   For Southern rights will do.
> We've sent the bravest of our land
>   To battle with the foe,
> And we will lend a helping hand;
>   We love the South, you know.
>
>   Hurrah! hurrah! etc.

WAKING UP THE BATTERIES.

Now, Northern goods are out of date;
   And since old Abe's blockade,
We, Southern girls can be content
   With goods that's Southern made.
We sent our sweethearts to the war,
   But, dear girls, never mind,
Your soldier-love will ne'er forget
   The girl he left behind.
      Hurrah! hurrah! etc.

The soldier is the lad for me—
   A brave heart I adore;
And when the sunny South is free,
   And fighting is no more,
I'll choose me then a lover brave
   From out the gallant band,
The soldier lad I love the best
   Shall have my heart and hand.
      Hurrah! hurrah! etc.

The Southern land's a glorious land,
   And has a glorious cause;
Then cheer, three cheers for Southern rights,
   And for the Southern boys.
We scorn to wear a bit of silk,
   A bit of Northern lace:
But make our homespun dresses up,
   And wear them with such grace.
      Hurrah! hurrah! etc.

And now, young man, a word to you;
   If you would win the fair,
Go to the field where honor calls,
   And win your lady there.
Remember that our brightest smiles
   Are for the true and brave,

And that our tears are all for those
Who fill a soldier's grave.

CHORUS.—Hurrah! hurrah!
For the sunny South so dear;
Hurrah for the homespun dress
The Southern ladies wear."

A tempest of applause succeeded, in the midst of which one of the soldiers shouted, "Three cheers for a Southern young lady who illustrates that song by herself wearing a homespun dress! God bless her, and give one like her to every home in Dixie!"

The whole mountain top rang with the enthusiastic cheers which followed; and Captain Ward then remarked:

"Gentlemen, it is needless to say that we are under a thousand obligations to our fair friend who has made this mountain peak seem like the home of the muses; or better far, like one of our sweet Southern homes; but as I wish her to enjoy the view over the surrounding country before dusk, we must bid you adieu."

Miss Harper then gracefully bowed to the throng, exclaiming in an audible tone, "God bless our Southern soldiers!"

All hats were lifted, and every one politely saluted them as the captain and his beautiful charge passed on from their midst.

The party then walked forward to the parapet, and looked upon the rolling hills, which bordered the base of the great mountain on the north.

For a while they stood, viewing the dark forests

WAKING UP THE BATTERIES. 121

below, with open areas of fields here and there. Peering out of the first or whitening the latter were the tents of the Federal army, in front of which, like little red threads, ran the entrenchments. Before even these they could in one spot and then another see little puffs of smoke and hear faint sounds of skirmish firing.

Just at this time Lieutenant Sam Kennard, of Guibor's battery came up, and, after saluting the party, remarked: "I see you are again taking a view over the Yankee camps and the surroundings in general. I have a copy of this morning's *Atlanta Intelligencer*, in which is a most beautiful description of it, and which I will let you have."

"Thank you very much," said Miss Harper, and Captain Ward, taking the paper, in compliance with her evident desire read the article, as they sat down under a small cedar tree.

"One of the most magnificent views to be seen on earth is the scene exhibited from the summit of the Kennesaw Mountain. From its base a valley on all sides spreads off in billowy-like surfaces, rolling higher and higher until it is lost on the south on the blue outline of the southeastern spur of the Alleghanies, on whose crests the white line of houses and occasional spires of Atlanta are plainly visible. Southward, beyond that regular line, a smooth, blue cone lifts up its head above all the ridges within view, and overlooks the eminences of all the country. It is Stone Mountain, that barren hill and wonderful curiosity that arises like a huge loaf, and, though over twenty miles south of the crests where Atlanta rests in her beauty, it seems as though it was a helmet sitting on the brow of this giant ridge.

"Eastward, and but a few miles from the base of the Kennesaw, the lovely village of Marietta gleams out from amid the luxuriant foliage which embowers it like an emerald setting woven in a cluster of diamonds. In its desolation it remains beautiful. Its arbored shades look as inviting as when the exquisite forms of beauty and the attractive eyes of lovely and loved women, and elegant people charmed the visitor to remain and luxuriate amid its endearments. The defacing touch and destroying presence of an army are evident on its face. Its citizens gone, its magnificent homes deserted, its regal residences desolate, its church bells quiet, its halls abandoned and its music silenced, it remains but a warlike citadel on the plain. The echoes of war, the fitful signal of the clanging, spurred dragoons, the challenge of the sentry, the snort of the war-horse, the shrieks of the steam-engines, the rumbling of trains of cars and long lines of wagons, and the shouts of teamsters and workmen, swell aloud on the air at intervals, and then the oppressive silence becomes more intolerable than the noise was before. The destructive finger of war is laid on the village, but it remains beautiful in its ruins. Northeastward from the slope of the mountain the billowy hills wave into the dim, misty outline of the crests whose thin blue brows stretch to the Catskills on the Hudson. The Blue Ridge, with all its strange contour and fantastic outlines, fades before us into a cloud, and into the impenetrable depths where even distance does not 'lend enchantment to the view,' by robing the 'mountain in its azure hue.'

"Brush Mountain casts up its shaggy head before us, and like the hump of a camel sits a ragged monster barrier, on whose sloping face an army

WAKING UP THE BATTERIES. 123

defends the pathways that lead to the goal of our enemy's ambition. At its feet a smiling, peaceful valley shows its fair face, and, laughing in the sunlight, its green fields and treasured homes reflect back the scorched rays of the bright sun, shining like the glorious gems that they are to the husbandman. Far off northward their bosoms are bared to grow the wealth that fills our granaries and storehouses with their golden grain. The limit is bounded by the hills along the Etowah. Skirting the horizon, their broken backs are misty and dim. Sometimes a dull red or barren sandy spot on the iron hills gleams out on their sides or summits.

"To the north and westward the fertile country presents a repetition of hills and valleys that are studded with the beautiful farms of planters, whose homes awhile since were busy hives of industry, and where peaceful sounds of pastoral life only broke on the ear.

"The great red banks of the Western & Atlantic Railroad wind like the tortuous curvings of a huge snake along over the surface—here on an enormous bank, there through a deep cut. It winds back and forth, binding the mountains and valleys with links of iron, and transports the treasures of the caverns on the Tennessee on its surface for the necessities and luxuries of a people hundreds of miles to the southward.

"Away over the tops of the peaked hills at Allatoona, the dim outlines of the ranges of hills along the Etowah and Oostanaula float in the mists of the quivering sunlight. We almost seem to see, bounding the horizon, and shutting off the view, the exquisitely beautiful and gracefully curved outlines of Lookout Mountain.

"The sparkling, glassy curves of Noonday Creek glitter in the sun's rays. But to-day, instead of the fairies that once sported beneath the silver sheen of the moon's soft rays, armed men make night hideous with their brawls, their hoarse challenges, and the quick, sharp shot of their deadly rifles.

"Off to the left, nearly in the track of the setting sun, Pine Mountain shows its sombre sides. Almost dark with the perennial verdure of its foliage, its cypress gloom frowns down black as a funeral pall. It mourns that a deed of blood and crime was done on its crown. There it stands, and forever will remain a monument for legends and history, to tell that a noble Christian, a gallant warrior, a great champion, and a loved man died in battle at the hands of our enemy. .There General Leonidas Polk, the great bishop, the great general, was killed. Even our enemies cannot rejoice over the horrid deed. Our country mourns his loss. History will weave about his crosier, his sword and his tomb, and entwine with the chaplet that adorns his memory, his many virtues and his glorious, gallant deeds.

"South of the dark mountain a black and gloomy forest presents its interminable and intricate labyrinths of trees. They are overlooked by Lost Mountain, which stands grim and frowning like a huge grizzly monarch of the olden time. The very air of antiquity seems to hang over it, and though a wonderful curiosity, a monstrous freak of nature's fantastic humor,* yet it stands a forbidding sentinel and landmark to the hundred hills around.

"South and west are the bloody depths about New Hope Church and Dallas. Eastward are the yet ghostlier places of sepulchre about Gilgal, and beyond the base of Little Kennesaw are seen the

---
*It is said that Lost Mountain was so called because it wandered away from all the other mountains and got lost.
From its summit one can easily look into Marietta, eight miles distant,

WAKING UP THE BATTERIES.

mazes of the dark and bloody grounds where battle has made fearful and horrid marks.

"Over the whole valley surrounding the base of Kennesaw the arts and appliances of war have displaced the humbler work of the husbandman. Interminable lengths of earthworks and forts, parallels and approaches, defenses and advance lines, batteries and muskets and warrior foes cover the land. Thousands of white spots declare the tented field. The deep-mouthed bellowing of brazen cannon, the chopping sound of the picket shots, volleys of opposing musketry, shouts of infuriated men, the yells of advancing foes, the neighing of the war steeds, the bray of mules, the shrill blasts of trumpets, the roars of mimic thunder, answering the furious bursts of the battle storm, the charge, the broken retreat, the cheer of the victors—all echo up to our perch on the crown of the giant that sits serene where no political tempest, no national convulsion or continental earthquake can shake its philosophic calm or its granite foundation. The smoke of battle rises thick and in fetid volumes. Hundreds of souls, the *manes* of the dead, are floating to the skies on that sulphurous vapor, and its incense arises from those battle-field altars of sacrifice, and the sun hides its face behind the white cloud, but tints the attenuated sheet with gorgeous colors. Deep brown and red edges shade the purple mists, and faint patches of blue open like gateways to the fair and glorious heaven beyond.

"The battle still rages and roars its puny thunderstrokes against the battlement that stretches its rocky crest far up into God's own bright sky. A violet glory rests over the western horizon. Dim stretches of gold radiate from the far-off mountains to the o'erarching zenith, crimson spots paint and mottle the dim sapphire glow that casts its glorious mantle over the earth. The gorgeous scene slowly faints away beneath the sun's dying rays. 'Tis sunset.

"Twilight comes on apace, and night. Then the moon glides up the sky and over the mountain, and looks down on a scene of blood, where proud mortals cast the lives and pride of a province away. It coldly frowns on the battle-field. It sadly smiles on Kennesaw."

"That is indeed beautiful!" exclaimed Miss Harper, "and how true, too."

"Yes," replied Captain Ward, "it is a very fine piece of word painting.* But ah! listen."

In the still summer air, just before twilight, they could hear the brass bands of the Federal army playing the national airs, some "Hail Columbia, happy land!" and others, "The star-spangled banner, oh, long may it wave!"

"Yes," exclaimed Miss Harper, after a pause, "I wish we could hail Columbia as a happy land; but we can't do it until our country's soil is free

---

*Another very graphic description of this imposing scene is found in the following extract from a letter by the correspondent of the "Atlanta Register," published during June, 1864:

"Our object being to visit the mountain, we did not tarry long in the city, which one can scarcely recognize as the quiet little watering place of years gone by.

* * * It is three miles to the top of Kennesaw Mountain, which looms up so plainly as you leave the city (Marietta) that you would hardly imagine it half the distance.

* * * Thought it wouldn't do to stand still, and kept on up towards the mountain top. Hadn't gone far before another wicked shell went crashing through the trees overhead, and we went down again. Got up again, however, and traveled along the rocky path at a very lively pace, until we ensconced ourself behind the works of the battery at the apex. After a little while, our ears becoming less nice, we strolled outside of the battery, and took a good view of the Army of the Cumberland spread out before us in the valley below. It was a grand sight, and one worth risking more shells than the Yankees can throw at Kennesaw to see. In the distance the plains were dotted with Yankee tents and wagons, here and

MRS. HARPER'S HOME.

from the invader's tread; when it is, we can salute her in pæans of joy and triumph."

"Ah!" said Captain Ward, "the Yankees say the Southern women do more to bolster up the Confederacy by their tongues than the men do by their arms. I see you are a true Southern woman!"

"Yes, and I shall always remain so!" said his fair comrade, "but listen to that Yankee band playing the 'Star-spangled banner.' They appropriate a Southern man's poetry just as they appropriate our homes and our stores. And see those thousands of tents of our enemies on Georgia soil. Oh! let us go away from here; it makes me angry to look at them; if I stay I shall think and say what I ought not. Come, Jack, we must return to Marietta."

"Well, I will go with you," said Captain Ward, "and Minon, also, of course. I would detail Minon for the special service; but he is not in condition to

there, like little villages of Southern negro quarters; and nearer their lines and fortifications were plainly visible, apparently not over a mile distant.

With the aid of a glass we could see the gunners plainly as they loaded their pieces, and nearer still could be discerned plainly with the naked eye their sharpshooters down lower in the valley, popping away now and then at our men. On Little Kennesaw, to our left, a battery of our guns was firing away at the Yankee battery farther down to the left, and along both lines, as far as we could see puffs of white smoke were ascending from time to time, followed by the dull booming of cannon.

The smoke of the Yankee locomotives on the Western & Atlantic Railroad went trailing along the tree tops, and their wagons could be seen moving down towards the left of our line. We spent some time in looking over the shoulder of a soldier, who, with paper resting on an idle gun, was sketching the scene as it lay, like a picture, spread out before him.

It was hard to leave this mountain top, and the grand view which it gives; but we clambered down the steep, rocky path, dodging, it is true, as we came in full range of the shells again, until we reached our horse, which we mounted, and waded back again through the mud to Marietta.

WAKING UP THE BATTERIES.

help you down the steep side of the mountain. We will not go over to Great Kennesaw; but will take this military trail down the ravine on the south, between the two peaks, and I can arrange at the foot of the mountain to send you in an ambulance to Marietta. We had better go before it gets dark."

"Yes, we had better go at once," replied Miss Harper; "we ought never to have come."

"Ah! don't say that," said Captain Ward, "for if you hadn't come one of the pleasantest episodes of a Southern soldier's life would have been unknown to me."

"Then I withdraw the remark, because of the mutual pleasure which has been allowed us even in the midst of so many scenes of terror," answered the young lady with a smile.

Just as they were turning to leave, they were suddenly thrilled by the sound of a brass band but a short distance from them, which had struck up the inspiring notes of "Dixie."·

It seemed as though the Yankee musical challenge met as quick and defiant response as had the challenge from their cannon during the day. High above the calm atmosphere around the mountain top the glorious sound arose, and sent a feeling of ecstasy into the spirit of every one who heard.

"Hurrah!" yelled Jack, throwing his cap fully ten feet into the air, "Hurrah for our brass band!" and then the soldiers seeing his enthusiastic caper, joined and raised a similar shout. Almost like lightning it ran down the whole line, and tremendous yells arose from the entire division which covered the mountain.

As one of the soldiers exclaimed, "It's almost the same as if some one had have jumped a rabbit in the midst of the camp."

The band continued playing, amid the uproarious shouts of the soldiery, and soon finished the air, "Dixie;" and turned to that of "The bonnie blue flag."

"That is good," said Captain Ward, " 'Dixie' is more than a match for 'Hail Columbia,' and 'The bonnie blue flag' can cap 'The star-spangled banner' any day."

And now again the wild and piercing "rebel yell" arose above the mountain top. This was echoed back from the hills below by the cheering of the Federal soldiery, and thousands of them could be heard joining the general shout which was sent to meet the defiant "ear splitters" of the Confederates on the mountain. Then from Walker's Confederate division on the south a prolonged yell sprang forth which ran down the line till it was taken up by Bate's men in gray. Onward and onward it rolled its wild billows of sound until "faint from farther distance borne," it died away in a short, sharp whoop from Cleburne's heroes.

For several minutes this continued on the summit, until Captain Ward began really to get apprehensive that some of the Yankee gunners might open fire again, in order to make the scene livelier

WAKING UP THE BATTERIES. 131

in other respects than that of sound. But his fears were groundless, for they as well as the Confederates seemed to have concluded that there might be a truce for awhile between the cannon.

But after the vociferous uproar had subsided, suddenly the band on the summit of the mountain began playing, "Home, sweet home!" and, what a wonderful change ensued from the noisy demonstration which had followed the playing of the military airs!

An impressive calm seemed to settle over the entire mountain and forests below. The change was so sudden, and all the surroundings made it so touching that Miss Harper found tears gushing from her eyes.

"Oh, Captain Ward," she exclaimed, "you must pardon me; but how I do wish that this war was over, and that all of our dear boys were again around their firesides at their own sweet homes! Oh! would that I could look down the vista of years to the time when the bells of mercy shall toll the knell of departed wrath!"

"Beautiful words, well said! I cannot blame a lady for her tears when I find one dropping from my own eye," exclaimed Captain Ward. "Ah! when this war is over, may there be less woe amid the homes in the south and the north than I have sometimes considered there would be."

Jack came forward and took his sister's hand, and whispered, "Sis, just look and see how those soldiers are crying. I didn't think they would be so sorry to hear 'Home, sweet home!' played. I like to hear it. I think it's a pretty tune."

There was deep silence everywhere, except the soft, sweet music from the band; and when this ended, there followed for a few seconds a stillness as of death; and then, from far down among the Federal works was faintly heard the shout:

"When this cruel war is over,
Then we'll all come home again."

From thousands of throats it seemed to rise, and then from the Confederate ranks amid the cloud-swept crags was sent forth the good-humored refrain:

"Yes, we'll all come home again!"

Ah! the immortal brotherhood of man. Oceans may separate the persons, time may turn the hair gray, bend the stout form and dim the lustre of the eyes, hate may for an interval make them as tigers, striving to rend to pieces and lap each other's blood; but let the still, small voice of sympathy speak to them in the quiet moments, when passion's wildest fury is spent, and they would cast aside the deadliest weapons of wrath and clasp hands as children around their mother's knees.

Minon now remarked, "Well, Miss Harper, and Captain Ward, I think we had better go before it gets too dark."

"That's so," said Miss Harper, "let us go at once."

The party then, under Captain Ward's leadership, walked along the crest until they reached the slope

WAKING UP THE BATTERIES.   133

leading down into the ravine, and there began the descent.

They passed among the files of soldiers who were cooking their supper, or sitting down in groups among the crags, laughing and talking, and some of them reading their favorite newspaper, "The Rebel," which, originally published in Chattanooga, had been refugeeing before the army, stopping for a while in Marietta.

Sitting apart from these, on a rock, was Ward Childs, a nineteen-year-old soldier boy from Missouri, a member of Guibor's battery. He was writing in his diary, and sad was his heart as his hand pencilled the words that under the terrific fire that day Caldwell Dunlap, brave fellow, had lost his left arm, and that Bob Welch and J. B. O'Reilly were also badly wounded. Childs was a bright young soldier, and a general favorite.

Major Storrs was among the others, helping Pat Quinn to broil some ham. The major, when off duty, was always one of the boys, consequently he made a personal friend of each of them. Seeing the young lady, he immediately came forward and shook hands with her, saying, "I was just starting a few minutes ago to hunt you up when I was informed that Captain Ward was with you; and as there is no one more competent than he to give you every attention I remained back in the ranks; but permit me now to express my most hearty congratulations that you passed safely through what was really quite an ordeal to veteran soldiers.

I hope I shall meet you again, but I should hardly wish it were here. And, by the way, General French has gone over to the extreme right of the line. He said he hoped to see you before you went down; but that in case he did not, asked me if I met you to extend to you his congratulations at not being hurt to-day and also his sincere good wishes."

"Thank you so much, Major, for your kind words of congratulation, and for a like message from General French," answered Miss Harper. "But does n't it really seem too wicked to profane so beautiful a place as this grand mountain top with the blood seeking missiles of hate and death? Our noble old Kennesaw ought to have been left to smile down on perpetual scenes of peace and happiness. Ah! the Yankees, the home destroying Yankees!"

"Yes, it really does," answered the Major; "and you will appreciate the comparison when I say that your remarks remind me of a humorous scene which occurred when we were fighting before Cassville. Captain Hoskins, some of whose guns you see right behind you, had taken position on an eminence in an open space in somebody's front yard.

"Just as they had gotten everything about ready for the fray the old lady of the house came out, and said to the captain, in a shrill and very severe tone: 'I think that things has come to a pretty pass when soldiers has to fetch their horses and cannons right up into a body's front yard for a fight.'

"And she stayed there, complaining, until our guns opened and the enemy's shells began to whiz by,

WAKING UP THE BATTERIES.

then she, unlike you, ran down the hill and into the woods out of sight."

"Well," answered Miss Harper, with a merry laugh, "I don't know that I was so very much unlike the old lady after all; for the only reason I didn't run down the hill and far away was because they would n't let me. I will have to admit that I was in mortal terror for several hours."

"Yes, but I saw you run right into the midst of a fire so severe that the bravest soldiers quailed before its deadly fury," said the major. "Few heroines have done the like."

"Ah! it was not heroism, but the responsibility of love that forced me to do that," exclaimed the young lady with a shudder at the terrible remembrance, and with a serious shake of her head at Jack.

"Well, we put the flag up again, anyhow," said Jack.

"That's true, Jack, you put the flag up again in a very brave manner," said the major, patting him on the head. "I wish we had more grown men who would be as brave as you were."

After shaking hands with the major, again, the young lady and her escort passed along from the group of soldiers who were with Major Storrs.

All the others saluted the party with the courtesy, which is innate with the men of the South; and Miss Harper voiced her heart's sentiments when she said in an undertone to Captain Ward, "Oh! our Southern soldiers are gentlemen, as well heroes. God bless them!"

Down, down the steep sides of Kennesaw they wended their way, until at length, just as darkness was beginning to make the trail somewhat difficult to follow, they reached the level ground at the base.

Here they found several ambulances which had been sent to use in carrying the wounded men to Marietta.

Captain Ward put the party into one of these, and then exclaimed:

"Ah! I hear the tattoo beating on the mountain top. Farewell, Miss Harper, I sincerely trust that we may meet again under much more agreeable conditions.* God bless you for your presence to-day! Good bye, Jack, my dear boy, you are a hero already; live for your country and for God! Minon, I will see to it that you have a furlough

---

*To Captain Ward it was not vouchsafed to see the gratification of this wish, as the following will show:

* * * "Captain Ward was killed at Atlanta. One morning just after breakfast I went to General Ector's headquarters, near the line at Atlanta. It was about three-fourths of a mile east of Ben Yancey's house and fish pond. The general said he would like for me to fire a few rounds at what he took to be new earthworks for more batteries in the enemy's line to the right of his front. Captain Ward's battery bore directly on these points, and I requested him to fire about a half dozen rounds. He did so. There was no reply from the new earthworks; but from other and distant points projectiles were, every few minutes, thrown near our line and over us into the city.

General Ector, Captain Ward and myself were walking leisurely to the rear, Ward having ceased firing, when Lieut. Cruse asked me to sign a pass for him to take his washing to the rear.

I half way sat down, and was signing my name when a spherical case, or shrapnel, from the long range guns of the enemy exploded just above the heads of Cruse and myself.

When I arose and handed the lieutenant his pass, to my astonishment I saw General Ector lying on the ground apparently struggling to rise. We ran to him and found his leg shattered at the knee. Litter-bearers with Major Redwine, of Henderson, Rusk Co., Texas, now dead, ran up and carried the general under an arbor at the breastworks.

I had not seen Captain Ward until the litter-bearers came up,

for at least two months. Go ahead to Marietta, driver!" and then, after a courteous wave of the hand, he turned and sought the way up the mountain again.

Miss Harper wiped the tears from her eyes and exclaimed: "There goes the perfect type of a Southern gentleman! God bless his noble soul!"

The clatter of the wheels of the ambulance enlivened the evening air, and within about a half hour's time the party had arrived at Miss Harper's home.

And what need be added here? The reader can guess the sequel. After the cruel war was over a noble husband and a beautiful and sweet bride— not unheard of by us—received the congratulations of scores of friends.

Among the decorations of the church were fern leaves gathered from the sides of Kennesaw Mountain.

then I noticed the captain also down. A ball from the shrapnel had lodged in his thigh It was too high up for the limb to be amputated, and he died a few days afterward.

Gen. Ector's leg was taken off. He practiced law in Texas for a number of years after the war; was elected Judge of the Court of Appeals, and filled the office with much credit to his integrity and legal ability.

Captain Ward was a man of remarkable nerve. I have seen him under trying circumstances, and he was always cool and his mind clear. He was perfectly calm for three days upon his deathbed. I sat by him much of the time, and at the request of Bishop Lay, of the Episcopal Church, wrote out for the benefit of the captain's wife and children an account of the manner of his death, and giving my testimony as an eye-witness to the high order of his patriotic and meritorious services."—Letter from Major Storrs to the author.

"JULY 27TH.—This morning when on the lines the enemy opened fire on Ward's battery, which was responded to on our part. As it was about ceasing a shell, exploding over the works, severely wounded General Ector in the left thigh, rendering amputation necessary, and wounded Captain John J. Ward, of the artillery, mortally. Captain Ward was a fine soldier, and his loss was severely felt.—From Gen. S. G. French's official report of operations in front of Atlanta.

Further on General French refers to Captain Ward as a "most estimable gentleman and gallant officer."

CHAPTER VIII.

Night came on at length, and the thick clouds which threatened another rain laid a pall of Egyptian darkness over the mountain and the entire country around. No moonbeam, not a single star's ray broke through the canopy of gloom overhead.

From Marietta on the south and from the Federal lines on the north not even the gigantic form of Kennesaw was visible.

But by those upon its two summits the lights in the windows of the beautiful little city were plainly observed, as were the headlights of a couple of locomotives which were coming on the railroad from Marietta up toward the Confederate entrenchments at the foot of the mountain, while a magnificent panorama greeted their eyes when they turned in the opposite direction.

Beginning east of the railroad and extending westward, in front of and apparently almost under the two peaks, thence bending and sweeping southward for miles, were the camp fires of the Federal army. It was hardly an exaggeration to say that ten thousand fires, like twinkling stars, blazed amid the camps of Sherman's hundred thousand veterans* on the hills and among the forests around and beneath them. The myriad lights dazzled their eyes; and, although they were widely scattered, yet the general trend was a continuous one, and the "milky way" seemed to have its counterpart in the new firmament which war had spread out below them.

Parallel to this, and separated from it at an average distance of hardly half a mile, were the Confederate camp fires. These, however, were more irregular and not half so many in number, their prettiest feature being the fires on the other peak of Kennesaw, northeastward of them, which blazed apparently amid air like a chain of veritable stars in the sky.

The prototype of these was found in the Federal camp fires on Lost Mountain, about six miles to the west, which, through the misty darkness, shone like a dimly discerned, but gigantic constellation.

"A wondrously magnificent spectacle, isn't it?" exclaimed General French to Generals Cockrell and Ector, as the three and a few others stood in an open space on a large rocky knob, just where the western end of Little Kennesaw began sloping downward, and from which point they could command an unobstructed view of the Federal line,

---

*"I think all will be ready in three (3) days. I will have nearly one hundred thousand (100,000) men."—Dispatch from Gen. Sherman to Gen. Grant, July 12, 1864.

This was fifteen days after the great battle of Kennesaw Mountain in which Sherman's army met a disastrous repulse, with heavy loss, consequently his numbers before the battle must have exceeded one hundred thousand men.

from the bright glare of the fires on the east and in front of them, to where they grew fainter, until, miles away, in the far south, their presence was indicated only by a luminous haze which filled the atmosphere above them.

"Beautiful! beautiful," exclaimed General Cockrell.

"What a pity that instead of the light of festive lamps it is the blaze of the torch of war!" added General French.

"And that it is war," said Major Storrs, "we hardly need further confirmatory evidence than to listen to that popping sound of the picket firing, which we can even now hear, and the occasional booming of cannon down on Hardee's front. Look yonder; you can see the little flashes from small arms, sometimes a hundred at once, and several times a minute from our batteries or the enemy's the blaze of fire from the artillery and the quick burst of light as the shell explodes. Even night fails to ensure a cessation of the work of killing."*

For sometime they stood surveying the panorama of splendors which engirdled the mountain, each seeming awed beyond the desire of speech.

Colonel Barry then remarked to the commander, "General, don't you think we would have the advantage if our batteries were to open upon them

---

* "The usual flank extension is going on. Troops on both sides move to left, and now the blue smoke of the musket discloses the line by day trending away, far away south toward the Chattahoochee, and by night it is marked at times by the red glow of the artillery amidst the spark-like flash of small arms that looks in the distance like innumerable fireflies."—From General French's Diary during June, 1864.

WAKING UP THE BATTERIES.

to-night? We could see exactly where to fire, and their aim would be literally in the air, as the night is too dark for them to even see the mountain, and their task would be like shooting at stars. They would have nothing to fire at, except the flash of our pieces, apparently away up in the heavens, and that would die away before they could sight their guns at it."

"I was just thinking," answered General French, "as to whether that would work. They might, while our attention was diverted by our artillery practice, attempt to storm our position under cover of the darkness. However, as a double precaution I think I will have you and General Cockrell to post two lines of skirmishers, one beyond the foot of the mountain, and the other—the regular one— about half way down, to guard against that contingency, and then let Major Storrs and his captains treat them to a display of falling stars."

"That is perfectly agreeable to us," exclaimed the major; "and now, while the infantry boys are taking position, I will go back and have our guns run forward in all the batteries, and make ready for a simultaneous discharge, when the signal is given. As those rascals down yonder are keeping our men awake just for pure devilment we will give them occasion to begin to do some lively dodging themselves."

"And we will arrange our part of it at once," said General Cockrell to Colonel Barry, "and will notify you very soon."

KENNESAW'S BOMBARDMENT.

"Well, gentlemen," said General Ector, "my picket line, which has been pushed down to the foot of the mountain as soon as darkness came on, as is the case every night, will protect me against surprise. But, by the way, General Cockrell, didn't the Yankee batteries worry you a good deal to-day down yonder on the hill?"

"Well, I should say they did," remarked General Cockrell. "As one of my artillerymen said, their fire was perfectly abominable. It swept the hill top like a tornado; and the only safety was in lying close in the trenches. It was even worse than it was the first day* we took position there. The ground is now almost completely obstructed by a

---

*A gentleman who was a member of Hoskins' battery, says of that day's events on the hill at the western end of Little Kennesaw: "About four o'clock, the same day, two rifle Parrott's of Hoskins' battery were drawn up the back way of this hill, and pulled around by hand, and put in position, in open view of the enemy, about half way up the hill, about forty feet back of Gen. Cockrell's lines, or works, which would make us shoot over the Missourians. [This open space of rock with huge bowlders scattered loosely over its surface is easily found by the visitor.—Author.]

The object, it was said, was to find the enemy. We opened fire, which was the first gun from Kennesaw.

We found them. The smoke had not cleared away from the guns before the enemy opened with at least thirty guns, and things went to pieces, while our men took shelter in the infantry pits of Cockrell's brigade; but not until two men were shot down, and a wheel taken away. This first fire in the valley killed two and wounded three men of Hoskins' battery. The enemy's fire ceased in about ten minutes, but it had made paths of destruction while it lasted.

Orders were then given for us to roll back the guns, which was done, after making some repairs; but the strange thing was that we were permitted to do this without being fired upon.

It reminded one of a bee gum, and no one was anxious to stir them up."

Probably the heaviest artillery fire at any one time by Sherman was here, and concentrated on so small a spot. Out of fifteen of our cannoniers with these two guns, eight either sleep among the neglected graves on Kennesaw, or are hobbling through life as cripples. The slight wounds were not counted, as an arm or leg must be gone to unfit our men for duty.—Letter from a member of Hoskins' battery to the Author.

WAKING UP THE BATTERIES. 143

tangle of boughs which their shells have torn from the trees."*

The party then separated, and orders were at once sent to all at interest.

Within a few minutes the "tramp, tramp, tramp" of about a couple of hundred men from each brigade echoed amid the crags, through the night air; and soon they disappeared in the forest, down the rugged steeps.

Major Storrs waited more than an hour, during which the guns had been placed in position, the ammunition distributed, and everything made fully ready for the work appointed for his batteries, and which the men were very eager for.

General French himself, also, personally went from one end of the ridge to the other, inspecting the arrangement of the artillery, and giving directions as to the execution of the plan, wherever the location called for different details. He likewise sent word to the Confederates on Great Kennesaw, of the proposed bombardment.

During the interim before "the ball was to open" the officers joined their several messes at supper. Major Storrs, however, "dropped in to take a snack," as he expressed it, with the boys of Hoskins' battery, who were at the big rock at the eastern end of the crest of Little Kennesaw. Carnes and Walker, of the division band, were there, the latter with a new

---

*June 25.— * * * "Went early to the left of my line; could not ride in rear of Hoskins' Battery, on account of the trees and limbs felled by the shells."—From General French's Diary during June, 1864.

song which he had found in the Atlanta *Daily Intelligencer*, published the day before.

By general request he sang this, Carnes playing his cornet, just before supper. The delicious melody of the instrument, combined with the rich baritone voice of the singer, afforded the hearers a treat which was all the more highly enjoyed when they realized what different kind of "music" they would soon be hearing. Though the singer has now passed away, though the newspaper which published the song no longer makes its daily appearance, though the banner and cause which inspired it are respectively furled and gone into history, the and under changed conditions is maintaining its glory and is still as dear to its children, and the song is as sacred to the heart now as then, and is here reproduced:

THEY ASK ME TO DESERT MY LAND.

During our imprisonment at Point Lookout, every prisoner was brought before an officer, and had several questions propounded him, among which was, "Do you wish to take the oath of allegiance?" which caused me to write these lines:

Air—Wait till the war, love, is over.

They ask me desert my land,
  Its history and glory,
Whose faith is penned sublimely grand,
  In thrilling epic story—
Whose strength is written on ploughed plains
  By war's red, fiery finger,
Where crushing battle-shocks and stains
  Of carnage ever linger.
Dear land, loved land, thou art my home forever.

ERRATUM.—On page 144, the first word of the fourteenth line should be "land" instead of "and," as printed.

WAKING UP THE BATTERIES.

They ask me to desert my land,
  Lee, Beauregard and Davis,
Bright names that fondest hopes have fanned,
  Bright heroes that will save us;
Johnston, Longstreet, Stuart, too,
  From them they would me sever,
And in my country's blood imbrue
  My hands—I answer, never!
Dear land, loved land, thou art my home forever.

They ask me to desert my land,
  My banner proud and peerless,
And charge no more with blade in hand
  Beside the brave and fearless—
Through battle clouds, 'mid fire and shell—
  Fair freedom's land defending,
And hearing despot's dying knell,
  With shouts of vict'ry blending.
Dear land, loved land, thou art my home forever.

They ask me to desert my land,
  My tie of country sever,
Affix a traitor's deed and brand
  Upon my name forever.
They do not know the heart that beats
  Beneath my bosom's swelling—
I'd rather, in my winding sheets,
  Sleep in my last clay dwelling.
Dear land, loved land, thou art my home forever.

They ask me to desert my land,
  To which my life is given,
And with my spirit fear to stand
  Within the court of Heaven.
Fair, sunny land you trusted me
  Amid the shock of battle—
My arm shall strike to set thee free,
  Again when cannons rattle,
Dear land, loved land, thou art my home forever.

                    J. J. Mc. C.

Ah! land of the South, thou hast been called "imperial land," and well thou meritest the title, for the iron of an empire's strength, and the gold of an empire's wealth, the marble of an empire's majesty and the harvests of an empire's life thou givest forth from thy bosom; and in thy myriad homes, by the rolling ocean, or amid plains mantled by the evergreen pines, or where the oaks cover the hills and quiet valleys, or upon the towering mountains, thou nurturest a race of the fairest women and the bravest men that e'er the sun shone on. But a nobler glory is thine. Thy throne is in the hearts of thy children.

The Briton's breast swells with pardonable pride as he stands ready to boast or to fight for merry England, the record of whose prowess has gone through a thousand years of toil or of warfare. The Russian, at the command of his sceptred tyrant, follows with blind devotion the banner of his grotesquely mis-named "holy Russia," regardless of whether that banner leads to the defense of her soil or the oppression of the weak. The German fills his speeches and his songs with praise of his "Fatherland," and then—leaves it for a freer country. The Frenchman glorifies each hill and valley of "la belle France," and his heart thrills with patriotic ecstasy, as he goes forth to do battle for her fame; but nowhere in all the world stands there a country whose children love it with such heart-brightening affection as do those of our sunny Southland. To their minds she is the Queen-land,

WAKING UP THE BATTERIES.

to their hearts she is the Mother-land, to their souls she is the God-favored land; and, though they have been falsely called traitors to a government whose laws have been mal-administered by unprincipled partisans, yet they stand true to her, to her traditions and her glory; and shame be upon the hand and heart of that one of her sons who would turn back when she called him!

At length couriers arrived from Colonels Thos. M. Carter and W. H. Clark who commanded the skirmish lines,—the latter having gone to the foot of the mountain and the former having stopped about half way down,—that they had relieved the pickets, and assumed the positions assigned them, and that the immediate neighborhood was free of the enemy.

General French, who had not gone down to his headquarters, which were near the foot of the mountain on the south, and who was eating supper with his staff behind a tremendous bowlder, (so that the light of the fire would not be observed by the Federals,) then remarked to Major Sanders, "Well, it is now twenty minutes past nine o'clock; tell Major Storrs to open fire from all the batteries exactly ten minutes from now. The signal will be the discharge of a musket from this point. Tell him to order the men to fire rapidly; but with as great precision as possible. We want to punish the enemy badly before they get ready to reply."

Major Sanders at once passed the orders to the

artillery captains, and within a few minutes returned and reported all ready.

The general then called Lieutenant Mothershead, who was talking to Colonel Young, and said, "Lieutenant, take that musket and fire it. It is loaded with a blank cartridge; but I hope its discharge will mean the utter confusion of the enemies of our country and her institutions."

"General, here goes for a little discharge which will rouse the entire Yankee army."

With that remark he aimed in the direction of the Federal camps and fired.

A bright flash ensued and the sharp report of the musket rang out amid the darkness.

For an instant afterward there was silence as of death, then like the burst of a thunder-cloud, almost simultaneously from nine cannon, darted sheets of flame which lit up the whole summit of Little Kennesaw and shot their glare athwart the mist which overhung Noonday valley and its boundary hills, and, immediately following, a deafening roar shook the very crags, and, with terrific reverberations, woke the country for a dozen miles around.

Its startling echoes had scarcely died away ere from thousands of throats a tremendous yell leaped, till even in Marietta it seemed that the whole mountain was alive.

This was caught up by those of the soldiers on Great Kennesaw, who were awake, and a sound

WAKING UP THE BATTERIES. 149

"as of many waters" swept onward and onward through the air around the grand peaks.

The next moment it was repeated by General French's division, who seemed almost wild with the thrilling enthusiasm. Officers and men sprang up and shouted as if mad, and, to cap the climax, several soldiers fired their muskets off into the air. The example was contagious, and from hundreds arose the cry "That's right; let's give 'em a regular Confederate salute!" and, grasping their guns, they began firing,—the rattling explosions coming now singly, then in bunches, finally in whole platoons, until pandemonium seemed turned loose on Kennesaw.

The star-like flashes from the countless muskets, to the eyes of those who saw it in Marietta and in the Confederate and Federal trenches on the south, presented a scene of wondrous brilliancy. Thousands of men in Cleburne's and Walker's divisions, and in the other Confederate divisions had directed their gaze toward the mountain as soon as the deafening reports of the first discharge had burst like thunder from the sky, and now, as the blaze of the cannon and the quick flashes of the musketry firing burst out of the gloom some of the soldiers exclaimed, "It is like myriads of fire-flies playing around shooting stars."

They watched the bombardment with intense interest,* although it was too dark for them to dis-

---

* "For the last three or four days (with the exception of to-day) there has been a furious artillery duel going on between our batteries on Kennesaw and the enemy's. We have a beautiful view of

tinguish the mountain, and the whole scene for the next few hours appeared like the play of fiery meteors in the heavens.

But the artillery battalion on Little Kennesaw wasted no time in cheering. They viewed the explosion of their first volley of shells, whose blaze lit up the forest wherever they fell, and then hastened back to their guns, and began executing with great zeal and energy the order to "fire rapidly."

Generals French, Ector, Cockrell, Colonels Young, Barry and Gates, and Majors Storrs, Sanders and several others took position on top of a tremendous bowlder to note the effect of the bombardment from their batteries.

Of course, through the intense darkness no movement of the Federals could be observed; and therefore the principal interest was in watching the play of their own fire.

For some minutes they stood, noticing the bright light which would here and there suddenly dart forth among or above the steady blaze of the Federal camp fires.

Soon, however, the latter began disappearing, first one, then another, then scores, and the veil of darkness was gradually being drawn over the entire prospect below them on the north.

<small>the mountain from our position, and amuse ourselves watching the enemy's shells burst on the mountain, and see our guns reply to the enemy's. They have been firing frequently after dark. Then it is a beautiful sight to see the shells burst, and the long stream of fire from our guns when they fire."—Letter from a soldier in Walker's division, dated June 26, 1864, and printed in Augusta Constitutionalist, July 1, 1864.</small>

WAKING UP THE BATTERIES.   151

"Ha! ha!" exclaimed Col. Gates, "our fire is becoming too close and hot for them; they are putting out their own."

"Yes," replied Col. Barry, "they want to give us as great uncertainty in aim as they will have at us."

"Never mind, gentlemen," said General French, "whenever they get to their guns, and settle down to business, they will do their best to knock some of Colonel Barry's 'stars' out of the Kennesaw heavens. But this is good work which is going on now; and by the time they can open all their batteries, and get the range of 'the stars' there will be a sorry tale for them to tell among their own luminaries. Keep it up, Major Storrs, I like the way those shells of yours are lighting up the darkness down yonder before us."

"Ah, this is superb!" answered the latter. "This practice is as fine as I ever saw at night. The Yankees will have been worried pretty badly before they are able to reply."

For fully five minutes this continued without interruption, during which the scene on the mountain top around them was one long to be remembered,—the flashes of the discharges lighting up the clouds of smoke, and the silhouettes of the men calling to mind the classic fables of the Cyclops forging the thunderbolts for Jove.

Suddenly General French, who had been ever and anon casting his eyes toward the crest of Great Kennesaw, without a word, touched Major Storrs and Colonel Gates on their shoulders, and then pointed to the east.

"Hurrah!" exclaimed the colonel, "Major Preston has again followed suit in the right way. We can always depend upon him to be on hand whenever his aid will do good."

Every one looked, and within a couple of minutes two bright flashes of light darted from the high summit, and, as they lit up the clouds around them of their own and the one whose discharge had been first seen by General French, their sharp, "boom! boom!" shook the air, and were plainly distinguished amid the roar of the guns immediately around the party.

The trail of the shells could be followed by the eye, as the sparks from the burning fuses were strung out behind them like a chain of shining beads, and then their successive explosions, near the Federal camps, told that the dogs of war were on a keen scent for human blood.

From the throngs of soldiers who lined the top of Little Kennesaw a deafening yell followed.

Their lusty cheering, however, had hardly ceased enlivening the darkness ere a quick flash and sharp, crashing sound about two hundred yards down the mountain side told them that the Federals had at length opened upon them.

"Aha! General," laughed Colonel Barry, "you observe they are trying to knock my 'stars' out of the Kennesaw sky; and, just as I told you, they can't see very well how to get the range."

WAKING UP THE BATTERIES. 153

"No!" replied General French, "we need not fear that they will write of us in their bulletins 'driven from their guns' for quite a number of minutes yet. Look! three of Captain Ward's pieces went off then at exactly the same instant; and yonder the shells have exploded fully a hundred yards apart each."

For about ten minutes thereafter there was a continued succession of stunning reports from the summits of Great and Little Kennesaw, as the Confederates maintained a rapid and vigorous bombardment upon the Federal positions, which were still easily located by the camp fires and other lights in their midst; and only the occasional explosion of an answering shell was seen or heard, and these were apparently fired rather wildly.

CHAPTER IX.

Suddenly, however, from the summit of Pine Mountain, northwest of Little Kennesaw, the Confederates perceived a sky-rocket ascending the heavens.

It hardly cleaved its glittering way upward, through the canopy of gloom, and exploded, scattering its thousand sparks in as many directions, ere from the hill behind Noonday creek, east of the Western & Atlantic Railroad, another was observed, climbing upward, upward, upward, through the drifting mists, and, like a child of the stars, seeking the zenith to join its parents in splendor.

Almost as high as the great peak it rushed; then, as it burst with a sharp report, the head of this messenger of fire seemed crowned with a galaxy of dazzling brilliants.

Its radiant sparks were still falling like a shower of gold, when from near the Hardage house, and from the Lattimer place, two others shot aloft, each dragging a chain of light behind it. Then from Brush Mountain westward to the Wallace farm and far to the south, the air seemed alive with blazing serpents, darting upward, hissing, leaving a trail of fire behind, and spitting baleful embers at the mountain, before the darkness breathed its chilling breath upon them and, dissolving in convulsive agonies, they sank from view.*

"Magnificent!" exclaimed General French, who with his comrades was looking, almost entranced with admiration, upon the awe-inspiring scene, "I have never beheld so grand a spectacular drama as this which is rising from behind and amid the myriad footlights down before us."

"Yes," replied Major Storrs, "but our artillery is throwing some of war's most poisonous bouquets under the noses of those who seek to terrify us by its display."

"The majesty on high!" ejaculated Lieutenant Manning, "what a glittering panorama 'our friends, the enemy,' are exhibiting to us!"

"Oh, my! brother Manning," put in Lieutenant Mothershead, "here we've caught you at the theatre (of war); and,—who would have thought it?—looking at a spectacular drama, as General French calls it."

"Well, there's no ballet about it," said the preacher-lieutenant with a laugh, "so you'll make some allowance for me on that score."

*Some of the citizens of Marietta who were residing there during the siege state that these displays of fireworks occurred several nights before the great battle of June 27, and that on one or two occasions they were grand and magnificent beyond expression.

A gentleman, who was an officer in Sherman's army, has stated to the author that these fiery demonstrations were made for the purpose of alarming the Confederates with the apprehension that night attacks were imminent, and thus by disturbing their rest at night and constant fighting by day, to have them physically worn out by the time the great assault was made along the entire line.

"Yes, but I fear it means that there will soon be some bullet!" exclaimed Captain Canniff, with the French accent on the last syllable of his last word.

"Boom! boom! boom! boom!"—like the roll of the thunder of fate, from east to west the opening roar of Sherman's cannon broke upon the ear. In one grand volley, following the signal of the sky-rockets, they hurled forth a howling tempest of shells toward the crest of Little Kennesaw.

The next instant a shower of flashing lightnings seemed to dart forth from the midst of miniature greyish-colored clouds above the forests at the base of the mountain, or far up its sides, or beyond either end, and high in the air behind it, while the rattling din of their explosion echoed and re-echoed around the cliffs and clear back to the ears of the angry Federals who had sent them upward on their futile errand of wrath.

"Ha! ha! ha! ha!" "Whoopee!" "Try it again, Yanks!" "Shooting at the stars!" "Hurrah for the night!" and scores of similar expressions burst from the Confederates, as a peal of jolly and derisive laughter rang from one end of the long crest to the other, on perceiving that not one, out of probably fifty shells, had struck within a hundred yards of the parapets.

"What was it I said about their shooting at the stars, gentleman?" asked Colonel Barry with a comical emphasis of tone.

"Oh, you are the hero of the prophecy!" General French good-humoredly replied.

WAKING UP THE BATTERIES.

"Yes," said Major Storrs, "I think this will be a field night for us. We may not get much sleep for the next few hours; but I'll guarantee that our eyes will not be as red as theirs to-morrow morning. That was a grand pyrotechnic display they gave us a few minutes ago; but before we get through with this bombardment I opine their shells and ours will make a grander and more terrible one."

"That's so," exclaimed Pat Quinn, "I think the chances are that we are all going to get on a 'grand bum' to-night, and that there'll be a good many red eyes on both sides by daybreak."

"Well, we might draw straws," said Lieutenant Richardson,* "for who among us will make the best shots at that line of fire down before us; and the Yankees can toss coppers to guess at the one of their gunners who will explode his shell the farthest away from our perch up here. I'll bet a Confederate shin-plaster to a twenty-dollar gold piece that our firing will be twenty times as true as theirs."

"There's not much risk of that bet bankrupting you, Lieutenant, even if you lose it," interjected Lieutenant Cruse with a hearty laugh.

"Well, I'm willing to reverse it, then," said Richardson good-humoredly, "since you've caught on, and won't let me have all the chances."

During all this period the batteries on both crests

---

*Since the first eight forms of this book have been printed, a letter from a lady in Nashville, Tenn., who is well acquainted with Lieutenant Richardson (who is now a resident of that city,) informs the author that his name is Edwin R. Richardson, and not William Richardson. These two gentlemen are brothers, hence, probably the source of the error by our first informant.

of Kennesaw were maintaining a continuous shelling, and their missiles were flying, frequently with great precision, into the camps of the Federals.

The latter had by this time extinguished the greater portion of their fires; but the incessant flashes of light from the guns in all their batteries were reflected against the smoke, and afforded even a better mark for their enemy's aim than they previously enjoyed. To get the range of the nearest of these they, in some instances, depressed their guns considerably and reduced charges, while to reach the farthest they elevated their muzzles by sinking the trails into pits already dug behind them, which they ordinarily kept filled with rocks easy to remove.

The intense darkness of the night was the source of very great disadvantage to the Federals. They could not even see the mountain; and the blaze from the few guns the Confederates had, notwithstanding the zealous energy with which they were worked, was visible but two or three times a minute, and then apparently darting out from the sky, sometimes nearly a couple of hundred yards apart. There was no comparative object by which to locate their position, and Colonel Barry's remark was a very apt one, as they seemed literally like stars in the heavens; and so far as aiming at them was concerned, they were even worse than stars, for their flash, like lightning, was only seen for an instant at a time, and, before the piece could be sighted toward it, it had disappeared behind the clouds, and even the explosion of their own shells was no

WAKING UP THE BATTERIES.   159

accurate guide, as it was impossible to tell by looking at the flash whether it was near the Confederate guns or two hundred yards before or behind them.

KENNESAW'S BOMBARDMENT.

Still with the pluck and indomitable perseverance which are characteristic of the American soldier wherever found, they gamely returned the fire which was so annoying to them, and, from battery after battery, over a hundred guns hurled the hissing bolts of wrath against the mount of terrors.

As during the day, their attention was principally directed toward Little Kennesaw, and, as nearly as they could determine it, their missiles thundered around its crest.

Their aim, while at no time perfect in the darkness, nevertheless gradually became better, until by about eleven o'clock the bombardment reached its culmination, both as regarded its accuracy and magnitude.

Those who surveyed it from the crest of Great Kennesaw declared that it was impossible to describe the terrible beauty and majesty of the scene. It was a constantly changing panorama of splendors, whose magnificence awed while it fascinated.

The rapid succession of brilliant flashes out of the darkness which enveloped the other peak appeared as lightning darting from a monstrous chain of thunder clouds, while the tumultuous roar from their midst caused, as it were, the very mountain tself to quake.

But not here did the storm of warlike glories exhaust itself. The most resplendent spectacle it presented was in the meteor-like rush and the dazzling explosions of the scores and hundreds of shells which were poured forth from the Federal batteries far below them. As they rushed upward frequently the sparks from their fuses like fiery rainbows arched through the gloom, and, to use a soldier's words,—"each scattered a bag of gold," as it burst with blinding blaze and terrific detonations against the mountain side or high in the air above or beyond it.

"Look!" exclaimed Major Preston to General Reynolds, who was with him on the summit of the great crest, "it is like a shower of falling stars!"

"Yes," was the response, "and it is hardly more pernicious to our boys. The Yankees, somehow or other, don't seem to be able to get the range of the summit with any certainty. You see, nearly forty of their shells explode down against the slope, or pass over the ridge and light up the southern side, to where one strikes near the parapet. I have been watching the level of our guns as shown by the blaze when they fire, and that of the bursting of the enemy's shells. The honors to-night are clearly ours. The Yankee bombardment is simply a magnificent display."

"Ha! see that!" exclaimed Major Preston, "one of our shells and a Yankee Parrott shell met 'mid air and exploded almost simultaneously by concussion with each other. Such a scene isn't witnessed once for every ten thousand shells fired. Wasn't it a grand sight?"

"It was as brilliant as a collision between two sky-rockets," answered General Reynolds, "only it was more terrific."

In Marietta during this time hundreds of anxious citizens and soldiers crowded the streets and highest hills and the bridge over the railroad south of the depot, having been awakened by the astounding uproar of the artillery.

All eyes were turned toward Kennesaw Mountain, which was soon determined as the battle center, and with breathless interest they watched the incessant play of fire, apparently in the sky; but, as all knew, really upon the summit.

But at one point in the edge of town, at least, the signal of encouragement and of hearty "good cheer" was exhibited to the view of the dauntless heroes on the mountain top. This was at the Georgia Military Institute. The cadets were temporarily in reserve, and at their old headquarters in the college building, which was on a commanding hill on the southern border of Marietta.

For years the soldier boys had been trained up here; and from all parts of the state the flower of its young manhood had within these classic walls and under the noble trees, studied the upper branches of finished education, and been instructed thoroughly in the school of Mars, not only from books, but also by drilling on the college grounds and in open fields, where they were taught all the evolutions practised by the finished veteran.

This institution was the pride of the state, and yearly, at its "commencement" exercises, the beauty, culture and wealth of the state assembled here at Marietta to see the boys graduate. And not only from Georgia, but from the Carolinas, Florida, Alabama, Mississippi and other southern states came their wisdom, beauty and fashion to at-

WAKING UP THE BATTERIES. 163

tend these exercises; for from several southern states was the Institute's patronage drawn.

Governor Brown, of Georgia, always made it a special point to be personally present on "Commencement day;" and other governors before him gave it the official sanction of their presence. Ah! those were palmy days; shall their like ever be seen again?

When the step of the hostile invader was at length upon the soil of Georgia and the bullet and torch were doing their work of destroying the lives of her sons and the homes of her women and babes, the cadets threw aside their books, and, under their commander, Major F. W. Capers, went to the front. They took part in the desperate battles above Rome and at other points, and were afterward placed on detached duty of great importance.

Temporarily at their old quarters, when the first sounds of the firing echoed through the darkness of the night, the long roll of the drum (beaten by the diminutive old negro, Cornelius, whom every cadet remembers,) startled and called them to arms. Formed on the campus within a few minutes, amid the music of Cornelius' drum and pompous old black Charley's fife,* they beheld the play of the warlike fires around the summit of the mountain.

They stood in line for some time, and then, at the suggestion of several, by consent of their

---

* One of the former cadets, in talking to the author about the Institute, and the days when he was there, laughed very heartily about old Cornelius and Charley. The former, he said, was a small sized negro, pretty well up in years, and the very personification of dignity. He never met a cadet but that he gave him the military salute and always expected one in return. While thoroughly and almost oppressively deferential to the "seasoned cadets," Cornelius nevertheless considered himself really far supe-

commander, they broke ranks, and, hastening into the college building, and others, secured all the candles and lamps which were available, and soon had every window on the north side illuminated. Huge bonfires were also built in the open space in front of the main building, and thus the boys signaled their good wishes and applause to the gunners on Kennesaw.

Tom Bussey, who was noted for always having the cleanest gun of any of the cadets, and who is now engineer of the Marietta and Atlanta accommodation train of the Western and Atlantic Railroad, and as jolly and full of life as when he was in the Military Institute, ran into his room and got a sky-rocket, which he had been saving up for months. Coming into the yard, again, he touched it off, and up, up into the heavens, amid the cheers of the boys, it shot, leaving a stream of fire in its course.

This was first noticed by Major Storrs, who called General French's attention to it. Both readily surmised its meaning, and that of the illumination of the building and campus, and the major remarked, "I wish we had some way to show our high appreciation of their true soldierly greeting."

"I think," answered the general, "that the steady roar of your guns is all the evidence they want."

rior in wisdom and rank to one newly matriculated.
Old Charley was the antipode of Cornelius in size, being very tall and large; but even Cornelius could scarcely hold a candle to him in being pompous. When the wind from old Charley's expanded jaws went into that fife of his there was bound to be a sound which everybody around could hear. There is not a former cadet who does not smile when he remembers this universally petted and mportant old pair.

WAKING UP THE BATTERIES. 165

Others around them saw the lights, and soon from hundreds of throats went up the yell, "Hurrah for the Georgia soldier boys!"

While this was going on, not only from "College Hill," but also from every height in Marietta the soldiers and citizens could plainly see the enormous clouds of thick smoke which had clustered around the two crests, whenever the discharge of the Confederate guns would, like lightning, shoot a bright glare over the entire surface, gilding it with splendors, and reflecting back even into the valleys between the surrounding hills. Then the sudden flashes amid the sulphurous mists high in the air toward them, and the sharp, ringing reports would tell of the presence of the shells from the Federal batteries. Sometimes these would burst out singly, then a score of them, almost at the same instant, would light up the sky and deafen the ear with their angry explosions.

Occasionally one from a Parrott gun would fall in the very outskirts of the town, and, as its startling "boom" shook the atmosphere and rattled the windows around them, there would be a rush of the frightened citizens, ladies and children, from the neighborhood. Several of the death-dealing missiles landed as far as amid the grove in General Hansell's front yard, (now Mr. G. H. Camp's,) by the Western & Atlantic Railroad in the northern edge of the town. It was a night of terror in Marietta.

Thus until nearly midnight they stood surveying the awful magnificence of the scene, and listening to the tumult; and were congratulating themselves that the Yankee fire seemed sensibly slackening and the Confederates still held the mountain without great difficulty, when suddenly a cry of horror and amaze burst forth from nearly every tongue.

As from a volcano, a tremendous sheet of flame shot up into the air, lighting the clouds for miles around, and illumining the entire mountain. Then, as it faded away amid the darkness, a terrific crash smote the ears, and almost stampeded the crowd.

"What is it?" came from every lip.

"The mountain's blown up! We're ruined!" exclaimed a panic-stricken citizen.

"Oh, no! bosh!" retorted an officer, in a contemptuous tone, "a shell has exploded one of our artillery caissons. Our boys ain't frightened! Don't you hear them still firing? Only one battery is disabled. Hurrah for the Southern Confederacy!"

"Hurrah for the Southern Confederacy! The Yankees can't whip us! Listen at our cannon still firing on the top of Kennesaw!" yelled the crowd in a frenzy of enthusiasm.

A dreadful rumbling interrupted their shouts, and, with blanched cheeks, every one stood confounded with amazement and terror. Like the roll of thunder it came on, and amid the yells of thousands upon the mountain, a crashing, tearing sound told that ruin was rampant.

For almost two minutes this continued, and then, in the forest at the base of the great height, it died out, and stillness again enfolded everything for an instant.

The surmise of the officer in Marietta was nearly correct. A shell had fallen into an ammunition chest behind Captain Ward's battery, and exploded it with fearful display.

An enormous column of flame darted like lightning far up into the air above the mountain's crest, whirling the clouds like foot balls, and shooting its dazzling glare like a burst of daylight over the country for hundreds of yards around.

The whole of the gigantic mass of Kennesaw was wreathed in splendor, and for an instant the curtain of night was withdrawn from over Marietta and the Federal batteries, and they were revealed to the gaze of the men amid the crags,—the one smiling in classic beauty and the other smoking and frowning with grisly horrors.

Immediately accompanying the infernal flash a deafening roar rang out above the wildest tumult of battle, and, like an earthquake, shook the entire summit.

A tremendous bowlder was blown from its base, and hurled over the mountain side on the south. With a thunderous sound and with fearful velocity it rolled down the steep slope, knocking huge crags from their resting places, breaking tall trees like pipe stems and whirling them before it, crackling and whizzing, and like an Alpine avalanche gathering force and volume, until at length with a dull heavy moan it died away amid the night.

Another immense mass of rock, which jutted up nearly a dozen feet above the summit, was between the buried chest and the guns, the former having been placed there for the double purpose of being out of reach of the Federal shells and of being unable to damage the guns should any mishap explode it. The fatal missile which in part upset these calculations had struck a tree and glanced off at right angles, and darted into the chest.

The gigantic rock, however, sheltered the artillerymen from the effects of the calamity, and, although the dazzling flash almost blinded them, none of the men near the parapet were prostrated by the concussion or struck by the falling debris.

One man, however, who had gone for a charge, and had just lifted the cover off of the chest, was blown to pieces, and several of the infantry in the immediate vicinity were more or less hurt, but none seriously.

"It is the hand of God which has protected us who were around it!" exclaimed Lieutenant Manning, "let us render thanks for His wonderful grace."

"Yes," answered General French, "it is a special Providence."

Then as Generals French, Ector and Cockrell and Major Storrs, with a score of other leading officers and hundreds of men, who had rushed to the scene of the wreck, reverently bowed their heads, the noble "preacher-lieutenant," raised his hands, and, amid the thunders of guns from the crest before and

WAKING UP THE BATTERIES. 169

behind him,* and with the enemy's shells rending the air above him, prayed:

"God of battles! God of mercy! we thank Thee for this Thy mercy which has triumphed over the power of battle. Thy mercy is Thy delight and our glory! Over us this day Thou hast held the shield of Thy protection, and by Thy grace have we been saved. Grant that through this life the mountain of Thy salvation may be to our souls a greater place of refuge than to-day Thou hast made this mountain to our bodies. And now we ask Thy blessing upon our great commander and his chieftains, and upon every soldier, however humble, and that Thou wilt adorn our sunny country with the robes of prosperity, happiness and peace, and make it the center of worship, and of Thy glory here on earth; and to Thy holy name be all the praise, through Christ, our Redeemer. Amen!"

"Amen!" arose in a fervent tone from officers and men alike.

This had scarcely been said ere, like a curtain, the clouds above them separated, and the moon shot the splendor of her silvery rays upon the battle-crowned mountain and the smoking hills before it. The sulphurous fog, which clustered around the crest, it gilded with a brilliant whiteness which radiated upward again, filling the sky with a halo of iridescent glory.

---

* This noble son of the south was killed in the battle of Kennesaw Mountain four days after the occurrence herein described, as is shown in the following extract from General Cockrell's report:
"Lieutenant Archibald D. Manning, a minister of the Cumberland Presbyterian church and a most exemplary Christian, is among the killed"

Above the Federal batteries it appeared to spread a sheet of feathery down, and even the dark forests mirrored back its glittering beams from their myriad dew-sprayed leaves.

It seemed an ideal dream of ethereal beauty, the reflex of the smile of gracious heaven, revealed to inspire men's hearts with love for each other and reverence for God.

As if written in the sky, its lesson was one whose words to the soul whispered, "Peace on earth, good will to men!"

For a minute only this continued, then the drifting clouds rolled together again, and naught could be seen or heard but the baleful glare and angry hiss of the war-serpent.

Suddenly General French remarked: "Let everybody go to his post, and be prepared for any emergency. The Yankees are yelling in great triumph over what they think is a serious calamity to us, when really it is a misfortune merely local to this part of the line."

All listened attentively, and from far down in the darkness, from east to west, was heard the cheering of thousands of men.

"Huzza! huzza! huzza!" swept up from the abyss of gloom to the lofty perch on the mountain's crest.

"Here, General Cockrell," said General French, "I'll conscript you up here for a minute; and Colonel Barry and General Ector, form all your men, who are available, upon the summit, and give the Yankees a regular Confederate salute!"

"Yes, give them a salute!" arose from all sides.

The sound of bugles and the roll of drums were heard around the mountain top by even the Federals below, and thrilling even to them was this warlike music, coming at such a time and apparently out of the very thunder-clouds, or from amid the stars.

Within a few minutes nearly two thousand men stood in line along the ridge, facing the north, and then from Major Storrs' batteries all the cannon were simultaneously fired with an uproarious report, and the reverberations of their discharge and of the explosion of their shells below, had hardly died away ere from the three brigade commanders was heard the shout: "Make ready! take aim at the Yankees! FIRE!!"

From one end of the long summit to the other, with sharp, crashing reports which were almost co-ordinate in time, a blaze of fire burst forth from the entire division front, illumining the ridge as though it were crowned with lightning.

Succeeding this a wild and defiant yell arose from the men, and, ere the deafening echoes had subsided it was repeated again and yet again, until old Kennesaw seemed the house of uproar.

Of this demonstration a Federal officer, who was captured a few days later, said:

"When we saw the brilliant flash, and heard the startling sound of the explosion, we thought we had blown up your magazine; and the idea at once occurred to us that if we would make a rush in strong columns we could seize the mountain while your troops were in a state of demoralization; but when we listened to the boom of your artillery continuing almost without interruption, and within the next few minutes heard the blare of bugles and the roll of drums, calling the men to dress parade apparently up in the clouds a thousand feet above us, and saw the chain of musketry fire dart through the pitchy darkness from one end of the crest to the other, with a rattling din like thunder, and then were greeted by the infernal racket of your rebel yells, we knew that we had better stay where we were and let you alone; for no troops could be caught napping who recovered themselves so soon from the effects of a catastrophe such as we thought you had suffered. It was admirable; and told us a tale wonderfully creditable to your men."

The infantry demonstration having proven an entire success in restoring the *morale* of the soldiers, which the explosion had to some extent threatened to impair, General French issued orders for them to be again withdrawn to the southern side of the crest, out of reach of the Federal fire.

The bombardment, however, continued vigorously for about an hour longer, and then gradually lost force, until by two o'clock in the morning it ceased entirely; and, as the exhausted artillerymen sought rest in slumber, one of the grandest scenes of one of the mightiest wars of the century came to an end.

www.ingramcontent.com/pod-product-compliance
Lightning Source LLC
Chambersburg PA
CBHW020258170426
43202CB00008B/431